The
HUMAN
DESIGN
WORKBOOK

The HUMAN DESIGN WORKBOOK

A Step-by-Step Guide to Understanding Your Own Chart and How It Can Transform Your Life

KAREN CURRY PARKER

Hierophant publishing

Cover design by Adrian Morgan
Cover art by Shutterstock
Print book interior design by Frame25 Productions

All rights to the Human Design Body Graph images are held by John Yuill and Genetic
Matrix. For more information and to learn more about professional and advanced
Human Design software and training, please visit www.geneticmatrix.com.

Hierophant Publishing
San Antonio, TX
www.hierophantpublishing.com

If you are unable to order this book from your local bookseller,
you may order directly from the publisher.

Library of Congress Control Number: 2022910055
ISBN 978-1-950253-29-6
10 9 8 7 6 5 4 3 2 1

For my children and grandchildren. My prayer is that we keep healing the world and evolving ourselves so that we can better build a world of equitable, just, sustainable, and enduring peace.

CONTENTS

Publisher's Note:

Throughout this book, the author discusses a full-color personalized Human Design Chart. Because this book is printed in black and white, we encourage you to generate your own full-color, personalized Human Design Chart at https://humandesignworkbook.com/ for reference as you read.

INTRODUCTION

You were born a storyteller.

Storytelling is such a powerful creative medium that our brains are hardwired to learn about the world through stories from the moment we are born. We learn about values, morality, and motivation from the stories we hear safely tucked in our beds at night or curled up on our parents' laps.

You learn about who you are, your role in life, and what you are here to do from stories. While some of the stories you learned about the world and yourself were true, many of them were not.

As you grew, you began to master the art of telling your own story about who you are and why you are here. You wove together all the things you heard, information from the events you witnessed, and tales from your own experiences to create your personal narrative about yourself and the world.

The stories you tell yourself about your relationships, money, creative fulfillment, lifestyle, health, and even your spiritual connection all influence what you create in your life. The stories you tell about yourself come true and express themselves through your daily experiences in the world.

Your personal narrative sets the tone for your life experiences and for the direction your life takes you. However, this is not just about your own life. You are actually living a story within a bigger story—the story of humanity on planet Earth.

The story of humanity may seem a little suspenseful right now. Scientists are spinning some pretty grim models about the future of our world. Politics on a global level seem divisive and inequitable. We are fighting old, outdated systems that have left many of us feeling disempowered and devoid of hope.

Storytelling might not seem like much of an activist stand to take when it feels like the world is crumbling. However, your power to tell stories is the most radical and active thing you can do to change the world. Your personal story matters and is a vital component to changing the world in which we live.

It may seem that we aren't able to change the current reality, but if we begin to tell a different story and join our empowered stories together with the stories of others, we can begin to weave a template for a different reality. We can program our brains and minds to see new ways of creating. We can focus our awareness and see the elegant solutions needed to change the world. We can use the sensual nature of our creative essence and take the time to step out of the probable to manifest the improbable—miracles that promise to shift the world in which we live. But how exactly do we do that? With Human Design, a system that can help us manifest miracles to change the world.

What Is Human Design?

Human Design is an system of personality typing that is a synthesis of astrology, the Chinese *I Ching*, the Hindu chakra system, Jewish mysticism (Kabbalah), and quantum physics.

Human Design functions as a sort of personal blueprint (see Figure 1), showing each individual exactly how best to manifest their purpose in their lifetime. This system demonstrates the archetypal themes that teach us how to be human beings.

Your Human Design chart, which is generated using your birthday, birth time, and birthplace, is a powerful tool to help you begin the process of taking control of your personal narrative. It essentially functions as a map that tells you who you

THE HUMAN BLUEPRINT
THE BODY GRAPH

@KARENCURRYPARKER

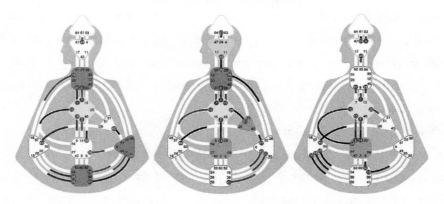

THIS BLUEPRINT SHOWS US EVERY ARCHETYPAL THEME OF WHAT IT MEANS TO BE A HUMAN BEING.

IT SHOWS US OUR POTENTIAL, PROVIDES ANSWERS TO OUR LONGING QUESTIONS AND GIVES US FULL PERMISSION TO STEP INTO OUR TRUTH, TO LIVE A LIFE UNMASKED, UNAPOLOGETICALLY IN THE REALNESS OF THE AUTHENTIC EXPRESSIONS OF OUR DIVINE AND INNATE NATURE.

Figure 1: The Human Design Blueprint.

are, how you experience and process the world, how you best make decisions, and what you need to do to stay in harmony with your authentic self.

Human Design is a cross-cultural, ancient, and modern index of all the traits that make us human. This assemblage of information gives you a systematic way to consciously explore your personal narrative and to change your current story into one of unlimited, empowered, authentic living.

Your Human Design will gift you with a new vocabulary, a new language to interpret a part of yourself that perhaps you've hidden away. Human Design not only gives you a new way of thinking about yourself but also a new way of talking about yourself.

The Aramaic word *abracadabra*, often associated with stage magic, means "I will create as I speak." Human Design is an ancient way of articulating an undeniable truth: Words have power. They can unify people. They transmit. Words are the bridge between the Divine and the human story. They translate the infinite into the finite. Words are the code for your personal story.

In this book, you're going to learn to use this new vocabulary of your authentic self to rewrite your personal story in a systematic way. Each section includes contemplations, journaling processes, and a template to help you craft a personal mission statement about your life.

Your new Human Design vocabulary will help you reconstruct your personal narrative so that it reflects your authentic identity. These new words have the power to change your relationship with money and with your family, friends, and partners, to help you find your right work in the world, to create more well-being in your life, to deepen your spiritual connection, and to heal ancestral memories.

Potential and Conditioning

Every element in the Human Design chart represents a potential—an archetype or theme (see Figure 2). Your potential can be expressed on a spectrum of possibility. You can either express a "high" potential or a "low" potential of all the parts of your chart.

For example, there's the potential of being a hermit. Hermit energy in its low expression can be a fear of connecting with others, causing someone to hide away, deny life, and never fulfill their potential of love and community. Hermit energy in its high expression can be experienced as the need to retreat to restore and replenish one's energy, to "hermit" oneself as a way of keeping their energy sustainable.

How you choose to express the themes or potentials of your Human Design depends, in part, on your conditioning. *Conditioning* is the way in which you've learned to behave in response to your life experiences, your family patterns and beliefs, and how you experience the energy of the world.

HUMAN DESIGN TEACHES YOU TO LOOK AT CHART (YOUR PERSONAL "MAP") AS A STORY.

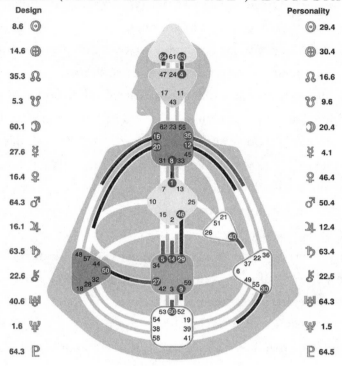

Figure 2: The Human Design chart.

Your personal narrative is deeply influenced by your conditioning. Your conditioning gives you a personal meaning that is associated with each of the themes in your Human Design chart. Unraveling these meanings can help you figure out why you may be stuck in a story that isn't serving the fulfillment of your highest potential. It can also provide you with profound insight into how you can consciously begin to choose a different response to life.

Let's look at an example. Close your eyes for a moment and think about the word *creativity*—a theme that is found in many places in the Human Design chart.

Creativity is a neutral concept. It simply means the ability to create something.

How you perceive the concept of creativity, your experiences of being "creative" in your life, and the beliefs you are conditioned by, influence how you express your own creative potential in your life.

Say, like all children, you are born with a deep connection to your natural creative ability. You spend your days daydreaming and thinking about all the things you'd love to do with your life. One day at school, while you are gazing out the window and imagining how it would feel to ride a horse, your teacher takes her ruler and bangs it loudly on your desk, startling you out of your daydream.

This experience leaves you so rattled that you consciously choose to not daydream ever again in school, shutting down a core element of your creative power.

Next, let's add that your parents are "practical" and believe that all dreams are born out of hard work. If you want to do fun, creative things with your life, you must earn the right to do them *after* you get your work done. Creativity is a luxury—one you can't afford. Your family's work ethic has conditioned you to place your creative dreams on the back burner in the hopes that someday you'll earn the right to manifest them into reality.

Finally, imagine that at sixteen years old you fall in love with literature. You were always a voracious reader, but as you mature and begin to really understand the elegance and power of the written word, you decide that you'd like to become a professional writer.

When you share your dream with your father, he replies that you are being impractical and that you'd better pick a more profitable and practical career path if you want to get anywhere in life. Reluctantly, you agree, and pursue a degree in business instead.

As a result of these conditioning experiences, whenever you think about pursuing your passion as an adult by being creative and fulfilling your creative urges, you suppress those desires. Sometimes, you think about writing when you retire. In your daily life, though, you refuse to give yourself the gift of fulfilling the full expression of your creativity.

Throughout your life, you are effectively telling yourself a story about who you are—what you're capable or incapable of doing or having, what you deserve. In this case, it's a story of someone who doesn't place a high value on their own creative expression, and they live their life accordingly.

This is the power of story. The words we tell ourselves help create our lives on multiple levels.

As you go through this book, you'll explore a new vocabulary that you can use to rewrite the story of your life. In addition, with the help of your Human Design chart, you're going to learn how to rewrite your story in a way that reflects the *true* story of who you really are. A story that represents the unique, vital, and irreplaceable role in the world that only *you* can fulfill.

I used creativity as an example for a couple reasons. First, many of us have experienced this kind of stifling conditioning regarding our own creativity. Second, in this book you will use a playful creative process in the rewriting your personal narrative. The exercises found here will support you in eliciting a response from the right side of your brain, helping you break out of the old, conditioned ways of thinking about yourself.

Changing your mind isn't easy—the brain has evolved to be a deeply efficient organ. Once you have a thought—or tell a story—multiple times, your brain begins to build a neural pathway that nerves can follow with little to no conscious thought. This pathway allows the brain to easily run the story through your mind repeatedly, even unconsciously, until it becomes a part of your identity.

This also explains why it's so hard to break a habit or create a new habit—because an old habit has become a neural pathway the brain reverts to easily, and to break that habit or create a new one you must build a new pathway for the new habit to take root. It requires time and repetition to reprogram the brain.

While we are on the topic of neural pathways, it's a good time to talk more about the biology of the brain. As you likely know, the brain has two halves, referred to as the left and right side of the brain, and each half is associated with different neurological processes.

The left side of the brain is where things like language, logic, and timekeeping take place. The left side of the brain predicts the future based on our understanding of the patterns from the past—this is what science is built upon. When certain experiments consistently give us a predictable outcome, we feel comfortable knowing that the pattern is true and that most of the time we can rely upon it to result in certain predictable outcomes.

The left side of the brain is also associated with fear and doubt, protective mechanisms that cause us to be skeptical and resistant to change as a way of protecting us from unknown and potentially unsafe things.

The right side of the brain is associated with the big picture. Holistic thinking, emotions, intuitive nudges, and traditional creative arts take shape here. This side of the brain isn't interested in logic and prediction, and because of this, it is thought to be the spirit of pattern-breaking thoughts.

Creativity, including creative storytelling, is associated with the right side of the brain as well. Every time you consciously tell yourself new stories about you, not only do you access the childlike side of your brain that is open to learning new ideas and values, you also draw on the emotional, intuitive side of your brain to use storytelling to break old patterns and chart a new path for your life.

A new story stretches your mind to begin thinking about new possibilities and leads you in new directions. The use of effective storytelling is well documented. Everyone from Olympic athletes to highly successful entrepreneurs—anyone at the top of their game—knows what success would mean for them, either big picture or small, and refines and focuses their vision of themselves living through that story. Our goal with this new story, which you will continue to refine throughout your life, is to write a clear creative vision. In this way, your new story can become a practical and powerful tool that works for you.

Getting Started

To begin your journey with Human Design, you'll want to get your personal Human Design chart. Note, there are several websites where you can run your chart, but you may find it difficult to match it up to this book. Some of the charts from different software platforms look a little different and sometimes have slightly different language than the terminology that you'll find in this book. While these other platforms may provide accurate charts, you can be certain that the chart you download from my website is accurate and free. To best follow along with this book, you'll need to generate your Human Design chart here: www.humandesignworkbook.com. To get your personal chart, you'll just need to enter the day, time, and location of your birth. Then download your unique chart, and you're ready to start working through the chapters.

Note: Please keep in mind that many terms on the Human Design chart can have interchangeable names; these are explained and illustrated throughout this book.

In the following pages, you will use your Human Design chart to help interpret your current story as well as unearth the story of who you truly are.

To begin the process of rewriting your story, you will want to become aware of the old stories you've been telling yourself—your conditioning. The isn't intended to make you feel bad or revisit old pain, but as with many things in life, you have to know where you are now in order to craft a new direction forward.

I'm a big fan of journaling because writing things down can support the brain in building new neural pathways more efficiently. To this aim, each chapter includes contemplation questions and journaling prompts to help you explore your old narrative—and begin to build a new one based on the insights of your Human Design chart. You'll work through a variety of questions that pertain to each particular section of the chart, which will ultimately come together to form your Human Design Life Purpose Statement.

This powerful creative process of unpacking your story up to this point and building a new one may require a few weeks to complete. I invite you to take your time, making it a deliberate and intentional process. Although you are going to fill in your Life Purpose Statement using the information gained from this book, I encourage you to alter the vocabulary, when necessary, to make the statement your own.

Words are powerful—they create and build. The story you tell about yourself sets the tone and direction for your life. The process of consciously crafting your Life Purpose Statement is the beginning of understanding who you truly are and overcoming any life conditioning that has gotten in the way of expressing your unique self.

I also want to be clear that there are no right or wrong answers here. Engage with this process without judgment. Pay attention to any thoughts you might have about the process and/or your story as you create. Be gentle with yourself and use this process to draft a story that is big and juicy, that calls you forward and anchors you even when you don't feel like your current life is aligned with your authentic self. The process of rewriting your story is a huge step toward building a more authentic life.

If you get stuck at any point, I invite you to take a break. Go play. Go for a walk. Do whatever takes your mind off this work for the time being. There's a lot to mull over here, and that takes time.

For some of you, the words might not flow at first when writing your story. If that's the case, you can try turning this process into an art project, a fictional story, or even a poem. Many people have gone through this process and opted to integrate it with numerous creative expressions. One person even turned her Life Purpose Statement into a play!

What's the bottom line? This is your story. You are in charge of it, and you get to write it. It's the true story that you've felt in your heart your entire life. It's the story of the person you hoped you would grow into being in this lifetime. Savor this process and view it as a sacred reclaiming of your magnificent self!

By the time you reach the end of this book, you will have written your new story and your Life Purpose Statement. I encourage you to expand on it, using your own experiences and vocabulary to craft something that empowers and inspires you and gives you something to aspire to. Once your Life Purpose Statement feels good and aligned, I encourage you to print it up on nice paper and even frame it. You can incorporate reading it in your daily practice. (I like to read mine every morning before I start my day!)

Chapter 1

READING YOUR HUMAN DESIGN CHART

Your Human Design chart contains two distinctly different aspects: your soul purpose and your life purpose. Your *soul purpose* relates to growth and expansion. Our souls manifest on Earth to experience whatever they need to experience to add growth to the Universe.

Your *life purpose* is the story of who you are in this incarnation—this life. This story is encoded in your energy blueprint as well as in your genetic and epigenetic lineage. At the moment of your birth, your soul purpose integrates with your life purpose to create the once-in-a-lifetime event that is you!

In the course of our lives we often experience a struggle or challenges between the aspects of our soul purpose and our life purpose. These inner struggles are often "prescripted" into the story of life. Many people find that when they understand their Human Design, they gain a deeper understanding of their inner struggles. This awareness helps them gain new levels of self-mastery, so that they can fulfill their potential in a richer, more meaningful way.

The Human Design chart, also called a Body Graph, is a visual representation of the sum of human possibilities and energies. The entire archetype of humanity is contained within the structural framework of this chart. All the possibilities for the expression of being human appear here. The Body Graph shows us the different ways we love, lead, follow, learn, know, grow, and so much more!

Your unique chart says all these things about you and illustrates your best strategy for practical things like making money, having great relationships, being healthy, and staying creatively fulfilled. It helps you understand how you work and how to best make your life work for you. We will cover these practical strategies more as we move through the book.

Following is a sample Body Graph chart (see Figure 3). Your chart may look different, depending on the tool used to generate the chart and your unique

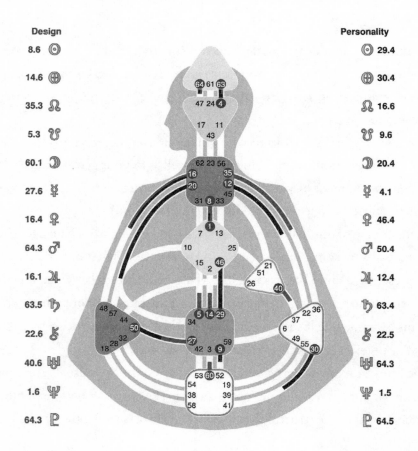

Figure 3: Example of a Body Graph.

expression represented within the chart. If you haven't downloaded your chart yet, I encourage you to do that now at www.humandesignworkbook.com.

Each individual chart, which is calculated using your birthday, birth time, and birthplace, is essentially a map of how you process energy. It reveals your strengths and potential weaknesses, in addition to your gifts and talents. Most importantly, the chart tells the story of who you are, why you are here, and how you can live a life that's true to you.

The story of your chart is the synthesis of everything found within it. In the following chapters, you're going to learn about how all the different parts of your chart work together to give you a richer understanding of your place and your purpose. Each chart story is unique, rich, and complex, and it involves *a lot* of data. The Human Design system is a combination of astrology, the *I Ching*, the Hindu chakra system, Kabbalah, and quantum physics.

If you study your chart closely, you might find some visual evidence of Human Design's influences. For example, if you turn the chart upside down, it looks very similar to the Tree of Life from Kabbalah (see Figure 4).

You might notice that sixty-four numbers appear on the Human Design chart. These numbers, called Gates, correlate with the sixty-four hexagrams from the *I Ching* (see Figure 5).

In addition, there are nine geometric shapes, known as Centers, on different parts of the body. These are similar to the seven energy centers of the Hindu chakra system (see Figure 6).

Although you can see pieces of these ancient wisdom teachings within the chart, Human Design is something fairly new and unique. It's a brand-new tool created help people in a brand-new way. (For more information on this, please refer to my book *Understanding Human Design*.)

Assembling all this information is key to understanding Human Design as well as each individual chart. At its root, Human Design is a tool that teaches us about the power and possibility of evolution in humankind. Knowledge can be

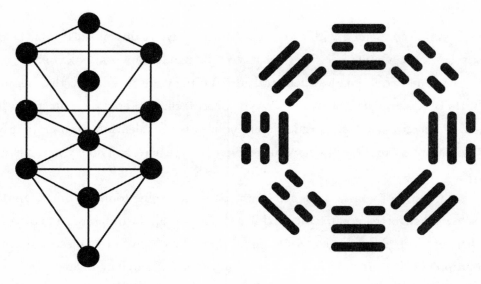

Figure 4: The Kabbalah Tree of Life.

Figure 5: The 64 hexagrams from the *I Ching*.

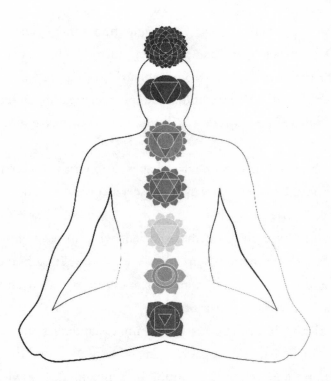

Figure 6: The seven energy centers of the Hindu chakra system.

found on personal, relationship, and collective levels. Human Design's real beauty is truly in the unification of all its unique esoteric components.

The actual chart itself is also a synthesis of several parts, which combine to provide an overview of each individual. To see the big picture of a chart and to make learning about Human Design easier, we must begin by taking the chart apart, piece by piece.

Breaking Down Your Human Design Chart

Let's break down the chart into its individual components so that you can begin to understand how these different pieces fit together. The purpose of this chapter is to give you a broad overview of the parts of your Human Design chart, so that you know where to find the information that you'll need for the rest of the book. The following chapters go into much greater detail, so think of this as an overview of the chart. You'll dive in deeper as you work through the workbook.

Some of the individual chart pieces have energies that are similar but are actually different on a subtle level. Please understand that as you learn about each part, we are taking pieces of the chart out of context. While every piece is important, the full expression of each one depends on what other elements are present in your unique chart.

Understanding yourself and the intricate subtleties of your chart is a beautiful and worthwhile process—and one that you could spend countless hours exploring, truly. For the purposes of this workbook and to make your storytelling as immediately useful and impactful as possible, some nuances and pieces of the chart will not be discussed in depth. We will cover the essential aspects of the Human Design chart, though:

- Energy Types and their related Strategies

- Profiles

- Energy Centers

- Planets and Gates

This will give you a solid basic understanding of your chart—enough to work through your new story—and if you choose to pursue Human Design in more depth I encourage you to read my book *Understanding Human Design*.

The Five Energy Types

When you look at the chart story/overview, you will note that your Type is the first thing listed. The Human Design system consists of five energy Types (see Figure 7), and each Type has a specific Strategy for making powerful decisions.

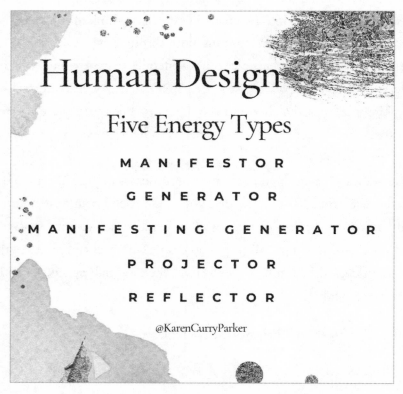

Figure 7: The five energy Types of the Human Design system.

THE HUMAN DESIGN WORKBOOK

The easiest way to begin benefiting from these Human Design concepts is to figure out your Type and to follow the Strategy for that specific Type. Each of the five personality Types has a unique Strategy for making decisions. Knowing your specific Type can help you develop confidence and trust in your capacity to make reliable decisions for yourself.

Here are the five Types:

- Manifestor

- Generator

- Manifesting Generator

- Projector

- Reflector

Each Type plays a different role when interacting with others and the world.

Strategies

Every Type has a unique way of making personal decisions and taking action in the world. This is known as a Strategy. Your Strategy stems from your specific Type and is perhaps the most important bit of knowledge to be gained from your Human Design chart. I say this because your Strategy provides you with key information about how to best operate in the world, including how to make the right choices for yourself and how to recognize when you are on the right path in life.

Following your Strategy increases your chances for fulfilling your life purpose and for experiencing events and circumstances that help you accomplish this on your path. Not following the Strategy for your Type can create further roadblocks and can slow your progress toward fulfilling your life's goals.

Given the importance of Strategy, you can be sure we will cover it in more detail throughout this book. But for now I want you to remember this: by following your Strategy, you will more naturally align with your life purpose; minimize resistance in your life; make strong, healthy decisions that will help you feel good; imbue your life with meaning; and bring more joy to your everyday adventures.

The Twelve Profiles

Twelve different personality Profiles, which are illustrated in Figure 8, can be found within the Human Design system. Notice that the Profiles can have interchangeable names, all of which are commonly used in Human Design.

Figure 8: The twelve personality Profiles.

THE HUMAN DESIGN WORKBOOK

Everyone comes into the world with a specific Profile and purpose. The twelve Profiles describe the major life themes that you will encounter, and they illustrate another way in which your personality interacts with the world. Knowing your Profile can help you recognize some of these major life themes as you move toward fulfilling your life purpose.

Each number found in a Profile has a specific meaning. The first number in your Profile is the element of your personality of which you are consciously aware. The second number in the Profile may be unconscious and more hidden from you.

Your Profile can be thought of as an explanation of your conscious and unconscious archetype and the themes associated with that archetype. Some people are aware of their unconscious Profile, but because it is unconscious they do not have much control over its expression.

The Six Profile Lines
Following are some basic definitions for each of the six Profile lines.

Line 1: The Investigator
The Investigator needs information and feels safe when they have sufficient data. (The internet was created for Line 1 Profiles.)

Line 2: The Hermit
Line 2 Profiles need alone time to integrate experiences and to reset their energy. The Hermit needs space to feel good and grounded. There is a certain magic to having a Line 2 in your Profile. Once you have taken time away, it's almost as if other people energetically perceive that you are ready to be invited out to do things and be a part of the community again. Your friends and family seem to always find you when you hide and will call you back out into life.

Line 3: The Experiential Learner

The Experiential Learner must experiment with their ideas and be allowed to make mistakes without judgment. There's no getting it wrong for the Line 3 Profiles, only figuring out what works based on their understanding of what doesn't work.

Line 4: The Opportunist

The Opportunist builds a foundation of friendships and needs to network as well as share. Line 4 Profiles need people to accept them for who they are; they need to know what's next and be prepared to feel safe. (Line 4 Profiles don't handle being in limbo well.)

Line 5: The Teacher

The Teacher is here to teach whatever they've experienced in life. They are considered karmic mirrors and are often subject to the projections of others. It's through relationships with Line 5 Profiles that others discover what they need to heal the most within themselves. Line 5 Profiles need to trust that you will see the truth about them to feel safe, and they sometimes hide their truth very deep when you first get to know them.

Line 6: The Role Model

The Role Model literally models for others what they are here to share and give the world. Line 6 Profiles need to "walk their talk." They travel through three distinct life phases: The first phase (birth until age thirty) is a youthful phase of experimentation and experiential learning. The second phase (ages thirty to fifty) is a long cycle of healing, growth, and studying. The final phase (over fifty) is a cycle of living what they've learned. Line 6 Profiles need to feel that what they are participating in is worth their effort in order to find meaning and energy in life.

The twelve Profiles are various combinations of two of each of these lines: Each Profile is a combination of a conscious line followed by an unconscious line. You'll learn much more about the Lines in your Profile in Chapter 3.

The Nine Energy Centers

The first thing you'll notice when you study your chart is that it contains nine geometric shapes (see Figure 9). These shapes are called the Centers. Each Center carries and manages a certain frequency of energy and relates to specific themes in our lives.

As you can see in Figure 9, these are the nine Centers:

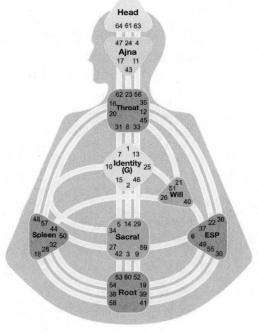

- Head

- Ajna

- Throat

- Identity (G)

- Will

- Spleen

- Sacral

- ESP (Emotional Solar Plexus)

Figure 9: The Nine Centers.

- Root

If a Center is shaded in or colored, it is a Defined Center (see Figure 10). A Defined Center has a consistent way of operating and is part of who you are—it's the energy that you radiate out into the world, consistent and truthful all the time.

It operates the same way both energetically and thematically. It could be raining, Mercury could be in retrograde, Mars could disappear from the solar system and your personality aspects would stay the same.

If a Center is white, it is Undefined or Open (see Figure 10). Open Centers are where we take in energy and information from the world around us and from other people. Undefined areas represent the inconsistent aspects of your personality. It's in these Open Centers that we have the potential to experience great wisdom but also pain and confusion. Not only do we absorb energies in our Open

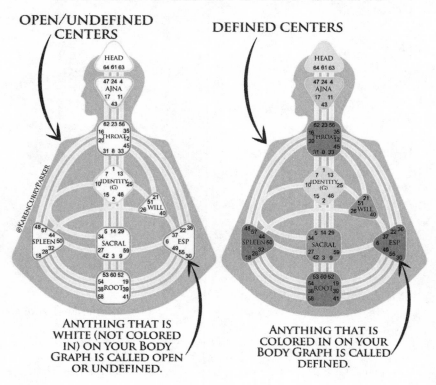

Figure 10: A shaded in or colored Center is a Defined Center;
a white Center is Open or Undefined.

Centers, we also amplify energies. Because we feel these energies so profoundly and intensely, it's easy to get overwhelmed.

For example, if you have an Undefined Emotional Solar Plexus (the triangle on the lower right side of the Body Graph), you absorb other people's emotions and feel them more intensely than the person who actually generated those feelings. Emotionally Undefined individuals are empathic. This empathy can become a great source of wisdom with awareness. (Any Center where you are Undefined is potentially a great source of wisdom.)

Let me give you another example. I have an Undefined Emotional Solar Plexus (ESP). I hate going to movies because I bawl my eyes out every time. When I watched the movie *Spirit: Stallion of the Cimarron* (an animated movie about a horse), I cried so hard that my then nine-year-old daughter moved to another seat in the theater because she was so embarrassed. Honestly, it wasn't even that sad a movie. What I now understand is that my Open ESP system was absorbing all the emotional energy in the theater and amplifying it. I was crying tears for everyone in the audience.

While not helpful when watching a movie, my Undefined solar plexus is a critical part of my life. In my coaching practice, this aspect of being emotionally Undefined is a great asset for understanding my clients' feelings. When I am assessing their emotional status, I know what they are feeling because I'm feeling it, too!

When I worked as a nurse, my Undefined solar plexus was overwhelming and exhausting because I didn't understand my Human Design. I burned out very quickly, soaking up all that emotional intensity. Now, I use my Emotional Solar Plexus as a screen, allowing all my environment's emotional information to pass through me. I don't hold on to it, and I don't become overwhelmed by it and burn out.

Children who are emotionally Undefined are sometimes labeled "dramatic." Yet, what they are simply doing is absorbing all the emotional energy from those around them and acting it out. I often see emotionally Undefined children labeled "disturbed" as well, when they are, in fact, acting out the emotional health of their family or even the emotional drama present in their parents' marriage.

The beauty in the Defined and Undefined Centers lies in the fact that individually we are all simply puzzle pieces—parts of a greater whole. We become completely Defined when we are together. We each bring pieces that energetically unify us all and offer us the opportunity to express the entirety of the human experience. You might sense this when you go to a restaurant or a coffee shop. The designs of the customers and the staff blend together to make a collective aura.

Your Definition comes from the position of the Gates and the planets at the moment of your birth. Wherever you have Open energy in your chart, you take it in from the collective aura of others. Your energy and your Definition (colored-in parts of your chart) interact with other people's energy and Definition. You experience other people's energies wherever you have Openness (white) in your chart.

The Numbers and Planets

On the chart's left side, or flanking either side (depending on your Human Design chart), you will find a series of red and black numbers in addition to planetary symbols (see Figure 11).

You might also notice that two birth dates are located on your chart (see Figure 12). (Note: On some charts your birthday might be set in the European format of day/month/year.)

The black birth date is your actual, conscious birthday (see Figure 13). It is also referred to as your conscious design, and it contains information about your soul purpose in life. Your chart's black elements are aspects of your personality that you are consciously aware of and, to a certain degree, can control.

The red birth date is approximately 88 astrological degrees from the moment of your birth, or roughly three months prior to your birth—when your mother may have noticed your movement in the womb (see Figure 14). This is your unconscious birthday, the parts of your chart about your life purpose and what you're here to learn. They are the design of your unconscious personality, the aspects of your personality that are consistently part of you but might not always be apparent. Your family and loved ones usually know the unconscious elements of who you are sooner than you will. Usually, with age, you become more aware of your unconscious personality, and you learn to fulfill your life purpose in a more mature way.

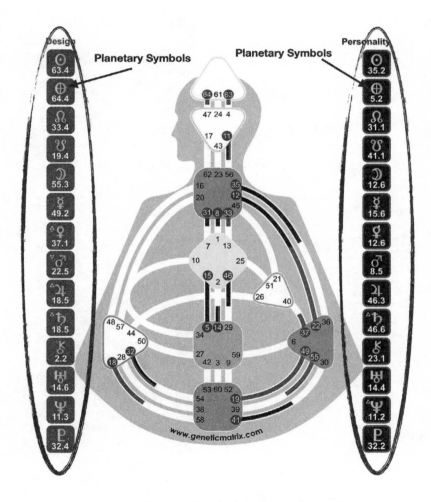

Figure 11: Planetary symbols in the Body Graph.

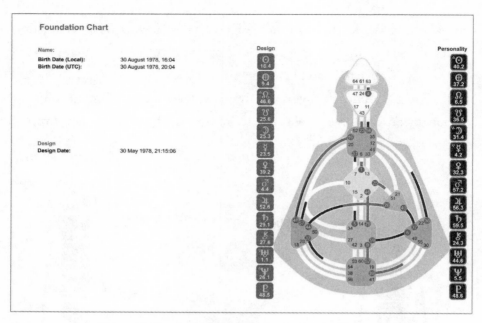

Figure 12: The two birth dates on the Body Chart.

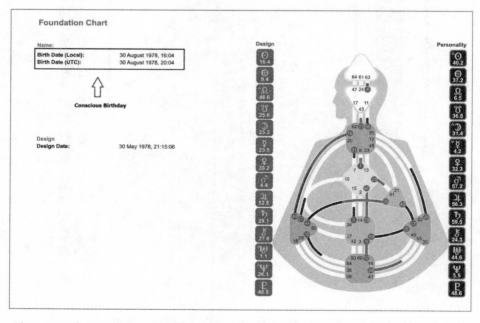

Figure 13: The conscious birthday (in black), also known as your conscious design.

THE HUMAN DESIGN WORKBOOK

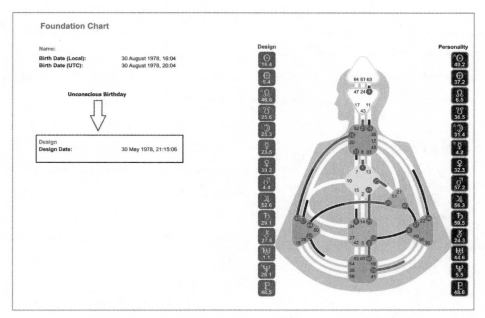

Figure 14: The unconscious birthday is also known as your design date, or the unconscious design of your personality.

Along with those black and red numbers you'll also find planetary symbols (see Figure 15). These symbols indicate the astrological position of the energies found in your Human Design chart at the moment of your birth. Your birth chart—the numbers alongside your Body Graph—is fixed throughout your life.

The Gates

You may notice that your Human Design Energy Centers are connected with lines; some are red or black, some are checkered black/red, and some are white. Remember that Gates that are colored in on your chart are Defined and part of your natural energy. Gates that are white are called Open and part of the energy you receive from others. Any lines that connect two Centers and are a combination of white, red, black, or checkered are known as Channels (see Figure 16). There are a total of 36 Channels (four of the Gates are used more than once in different Channels.) Each Channel has two Gates—the number where the Channel connects with that Center is the Gate. Each active Gate in your chart adds a different theme or "flavor" to your personality.

Black Gates are derived from the black numbers on your Body Graph. These Gates, of which you are consciously aware, provide you with information about your soul purpose. So, for example, if you have Gate 11 (whose theme centers around being a vessel of ideas) and this Gate is coming out of the Ajna Center toward the throat and is black, then you would be consciously aware that you have a lot of ideas. (We'll cover all the Gates and their themes in Chapter 5.)

PLANETARY SYMBOLS

⊙ SUN

⊕ EARTH

☊ NORTH NODE

☋ SOUTH NODE

☽ MOON

☿ MERCURY

♀ VENUS

♂ MARS

♃ JUPITER

♄ SATURN

⚷ CHIRON

♅ URANUS

♆ NEPTUNE

♇ PLUTO

Figure 15: The planetary symbols in your Body Graph.

Red Gates are derived from the red numbers on your Body Graph. They provide you with information about your life purpose. For example, if you have Gate 13, the Gate of the Witness, and it's red (unconscious), then you may not be aware that your energy field communicates to others that they are safe to share their secrets with you. You likely have no idea why people are always unexpectedly coming up to you and telling you their deepest, darkest secrets.

If you have checkered Gates, it means that those energies are part of both your soul and life purpose and are often a strong theme in your life. You express these personality aspects both in your conscious and unconscious Definition.

A white line to a Gate represents an Open Gate. You will always draw in the energy of that Open Gate from the world around you, and its expression through you will vary depending on your environment.

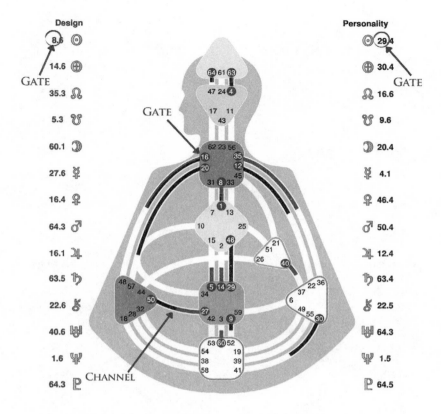

Figure 16: There are a total of 36 Channels (four of the Gates are used more than once in different Channels.) Each Channel has two Gates.

When you look at the numbers on the left side of the Body Graph (see Figure 17), you will see that each Gate's number has a smaller number next to it. For each Gate, there are six different lines, with each line being a further expression of your uniqueness. The lines of the Gates do not show up on the Body Graph, but their meaning can be revealed during a Human Design analysis. (Refer to the *I Ching* to gain more insight into each Gate.)

Conclusion

Each part of the Human Design chart provides key insights into your personality. Understanding these parts and the roles they play in your story will aid you in

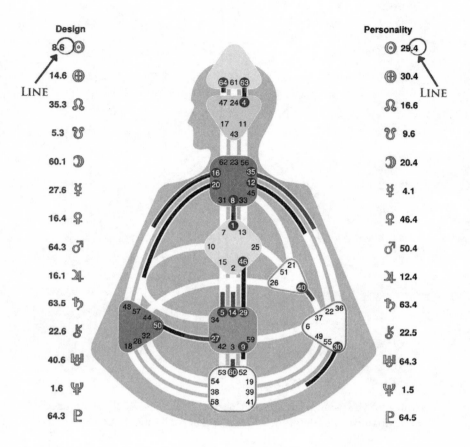

Design

8.6 ☉
14.6 ⊕
LINE
35.3 ♌
5.3 ☊
60.1 ☽
27.6 ☿
16.4 ♀
64.3 ♂
16.1 ♃
63.5 ♄
22.6 ⚷
40.6 ♅
1.6 ♆
64.3 ♇

Personality

☉ 29.4
⊕ 30.4
LINE
♌ 16.6
☊ 9.6
☽ 20.4
☿ 4.1
♀ 46.4
♂ 50.4
♃ 12.4
♄ 63.4
⚷ 22.5
♅ 64.3
♆ 1.5
♇ 64.5

Figure 17: Lines for each Gate.

assembling a bigger picture of who you truly are. While we must "take the chart apart" to discuss its key pieces, the chart's real beauty is in the synthesis of all the parts. The true story of who you are is only revealed when you bring all the pieces together as a whole.

Now that you're acquainted with the general pieces of your chart, let's examine each of these in greater detail, beginning with Types and Strategies.

Chapter 2

ENERGY TYPES AND STRATEGIES

Every story has a main character with their own personality, purpose, and challenges that eventually lead to the maturation of the character at the end of the story. There are five "main characters" in Human Design, which are called Types.

Understanding your Human Design Type tells you about your life purpose; how you create; how you best make decisions; and, through illuminating core themes about your life, how you can fulfill the potential of your authentic self. Knowing about your Type helps you define what you need in your life to stay connected to your authentic self, energized, and vital.

Close your eyes. Envision a bountiful, flowing river. That river is your abundance. To be in the flow of this river of abundance, you have many options: you can jump in, swim across, float on an inner tube, scoop water into buckets to carry home, cross via a bridge or stepping-stones . . . .

The energy of abundance is just like this river. It's steady, ample, fluid, and moving in an expansive way. There are infinite ways to enjoy this river. But to really get the most out of it, you must discover the way that is easiest and works best for you.

Maybe you've rented a Jet Ski but you discover that they're loud and hard to manage. You'd really rather be kayaking. You're not going to get the most out of the river. If you're trying to swim across but you don't have the strength and the endurance, being in the river might even kill you. The problem isn't that the river is dangerous or only accessible to an exclusive group of people; the problem is that you're trying to get into the river in a way that you don't enjoy and that isn't making the best use of your energy.

Abundance is like a song that is just waiting for a composer and musicians to come along to realize it. It's steady, consistent, and always accessible to us. But you must interface with your abundance in the way that's right for you.

For years, I've been teaching people that their thoughts, works, actions, and beliefs create their reality—that they determine how they interact with the flow of abundance. While this is true, it's only part of the story. There is more to aligning with the natural flow of abundance than just using your mind and creating out of your head.

You must also be aligned with your specific mechanical way of interfacing with the river of abundance. We all get into the flow of the river differently. For you to stay consistently and sustainably abundant, you have to be living true to your Human Design and your unique energy blueprint (see Figure 18).

There are many potential combinations in a Human Design chart, between Types, Centers, Profiles, Channels and Gates, and more.

You are a unique combination of all these elements. Understanding yourself and the subtleties of your chart is a beautiful and worthwhile process. But, in the name of keeping it simple, the most important (and easy) element that you need to know to help you activate the full nature of your abundance is your Human Design Type.

Each of the five Types has a special way of creating and experiencing abundance, with a different role, quality of energy, theme, and unique challenges. Your Human Design Type is the fundamental essence of your energy structure. It determines how you manifest as well as what you need to do to stay aligned with your abundance, your purpose, and more. When you live true to your Type,

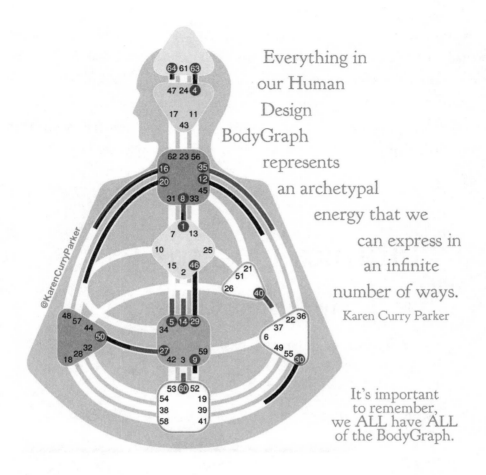

Everything in
our Human
Design
BodyGraph
represents
an archetypal
energy that we
can express in
an infinite
number of ways.

Karen Curry Parker

It's important
to remember,
we ALL have ALL
of the BodyGraph.

Figure 18: The Human Design Body Graph.

you create flow, experience opportunities, receive unexpected blessings, and take the right action.

Your Human Design Type carries a specific vibration that calls into your life the exact kinds of experiences you need to have to engage with your abundance in a way that is joyful and sustainable. But you must act in ways that are true to your Type in order to experience the full effect of your energetic vibration.

When we don't act or live true to our Type, it can actually push support away and make it challenging to step into the river of abundance that is waiting for us. So many times we think when things don't work out that we are "broken" or blocked. In reality, what I've found over the years is simply that we aren't accessing our abundance correctly. Following your Strategy according to your Human Design Type is all that's necessary to fix what seems to not be working (see Figure 19).

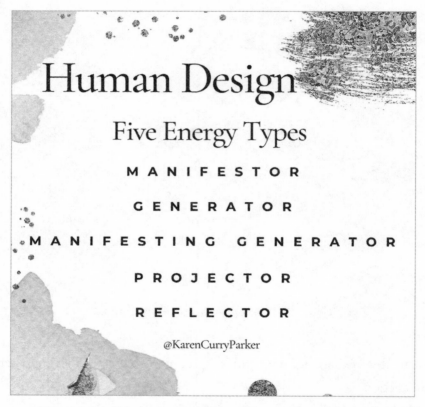

Figure 19: The five Types in the Human Design system.

Strategy

Every Type has its own personal Strategy, a unique way of making effective decisions and taking action in the world (see Figure 20). It gives you key information

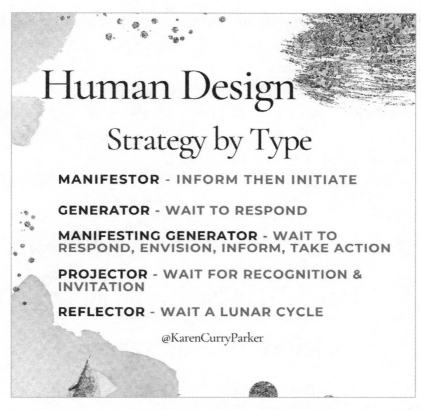

Figure 20: Your Strategy according to Type.

about how to operate in the world, how to make the right choices for you, and how to recognize when you are on the right path in life. Follow your Strategy, and you will more naturally align with your life purpose; minimize resistance in your life; make strong and healthy decisions that will feel good, more meaningful, and joyful; and truly fulfill your Personal Destiny. Following your Strategy offers you the opportunity to experience events and circumstances that are correct for you. Not following the Strategy for your Type brings events and experiences into your life that may not be correct for you.

Learning to follow your Strategy effectively can take months or years of practice. If you want to pursue the Human Design system, I'd suggest seeking out coaching from a Human Design analyst who can provide you with feedback and encouragement.

Authority

Authority influences what you need and, in some cases, the timing to use your Strategy effectively to help you make decisions. Depending on which software you use to generate your Human Design chart, there are various ways to talk about Authority (see Figure 21).

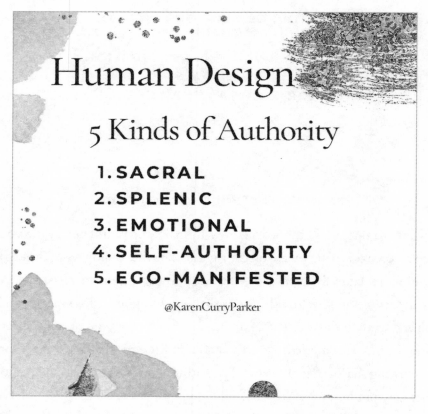

Figure 21: The five kinds of Authority in the Human Design chart.

THE HUMAN DESIGN WORKBOOK

1. Sacral Authority

All Generator Types have Sacral Authority. When you have Sacral Authority, it means that your gut response lets you know whether something is right for you or not. The biggest challenge with Sacral Authority is learning to trust your instinctual response. (To learn more about Sacral Authority, please read the Generator and Manifesting Generator sections.)

In the name of keeping it simple, there are four other basic kinds of Authority: Splenic Authority, Emotional Authority, Self-Authority, and Ego Authority. Different Human Design software programs will list other kinds of Authority, but these variations are simply subcategories of the four basic kinds of Authority.

2. Splenic Authority

Splenic Authority means that you are designed to know in the moment what feels right to you. Your Splenic response means that you can be spontaneous with your decisions. You don't need time to process or to contemplate. You will know what is true for you immediately.

Much like Sacral Authority, Splenic Authority is a gut-level sense of what feels right or aligned. For those who are not Generator Types, Splenic Authority can help you make smaller decisions about your daily life choices. Often, we master Splenic Authority in hindsight. Splenic Authority is that feeling of knowing something is right or wrong and realizing, upon reflection, that you should have listened to yourself. With practice, you can begin to notice your Splenic Authority in the moment, allowing the wisdom and awareness of your intuition to guide you and give you essential insights about what you need.

3. Emotional Authority

If you have Emotional Authority, you are not designed to be spontaneous. You need time to make decisions, and learning how to wait for clarity is essential to help you not experience disappointment or regret.

Emotional Authority can influence your Strategy as well. Your Strategy is still essential, but if you have Emotional Authority, it means you have to check in with your Strategy and sense how you feel over time.

When you have Emotional Authority, you are passionate and experience big feelings, depending on other aspects of your chart. This internal emotional energy makes it essential that you take your time to make decisions. It's easy to leap into things in the moment when they feel good only to wake up the next day doubting whether you made the right choice. Waiting for clarity helps avoid some of the regrets you may have experienced in your life.

Let's say you get invited to speak at an event sponsored by a group that you're not crazy about. You love speaking, but you don't necessarily enjoy this particular group. When you get the invitation, you're so excited to land a speaking gig that you immediately accept. The next morning you question your decision, and you worry about whether you did the right thing.

Over the next couple days you try to talk yourself into believing that you made the right choice. You manage to stir up some enthusiasm along the way, but you can't quite get your energy aligned with the opportunity. When you finally give the talk, several group members want to hire you—but they end up being clients you don't really enjoy, and you're left feeling obligated to continue doing business in a way that doesn't feel good.

If you had followed your Emotional Authority when you got invited to speak, you might have answered, "Thank you. This sounds like a lovely invitation. I need to check my calendar and get back to you. When do you need to know my response?" Your answer would have bought you time to really check in with your feelings to see if this was the right choice for you, and you would have been aligned with whatever felt correct.

The most important thing to remember with Emotional Authority is that your decision must stay consistent over time. If you feel a yes in response to an opportunity, that yes must remain true over the course of a couple of days. If you're all over the place with your feelings, it's not the right decision for you.

4. Self-Authority

Self-Authority is a catchall phrase for a few different, less common Authorities. If you have a chart that says Self-Projected Authority, No Authority, No Inner Authority, or Mental-Projected Authority, it simply means that you need to talk through your choices to gain clarity.

You don't need advice. You simply need a sounding board, a good friend, or someone you trust who can listen to you while you talk through your options. Self-Authority is common for Projectors and Reflectors.

5. Ego-Manifested Authority

Ego-Manifested Authority, or Ego Authority, means that you have a Defined Will Center and you don't have any of the other kinds of Authority.

Because the Will Center is about having sustainable energy and resources—or not—if you have Ego-Manifested Authority it means that you won't decide to do something unless you have the necessary energy or resources.

You must have healthy self-worth in order to be comfortable saying no to something. If you're in a pattern of trying to prove your worth by pleasing others, you may find that you have to strengthen your sense of value before you can truly follow the Authority of your Will Center.

Emotional Themes

Each Human Design Type has an emotional theme (on some chart versions it is identified as a Life Theme), which is simply part of a person's life and brings them lessons as well as opportunities for growth. When you experience your emotional theme in a strong way, it's usually a sign that you are not living true to yourself.

It's always good to take a step back and evaluate your life if you're feeling your emotional theme in a powerful way.

When you live your life according to your Human Design Strategy, you lessen the intensity of your experience with your emotional theme (see Figure 22). You might feel it here and there, but it won't be a roaring monster that dogs you day and night. Following your Strategy makes your entire life experience easier and more enjoyable.

Human Design

Emotional Theme by Type

MANIFESTOR - ANGER/PEACE

GENERATOR - FRUSTRATION/SATISFACTION

MANIFESTING GENERATOR - FRUSTRATION & ANGER/PEACE & SATISFACTION

PROJECTOR - BITTERNESS/SUCCESS

REFLECTOR - DISAPPOINTMENT/SURPRISE

@KarenCurryParker

Figure 22: Emotional themes by Type.

The emotional theme is thematic, meaning that you will either be experiencing the emotions of your theme yourself, or you may be experiencing them in other people around you who are responding to your behavior.

So, for example, if you are a Manifestor, you have an emotional theme of anger. A Manifestor has a Strategy of needing to inform people before they do things—a hard thing for a Manifestor. It can make a Manifestor feel a little angry that they must inform before they do, but they will experience a lot less anger directed at them if they inform first.

Breaking Down the Types

Now let's dive into an overview of the Types and their associated Strategies. Remember that you can find your Type and Strategy listed in your Human Design chart.

The Manifestor

Focus: Initiator, innovative, empowering, powerhouse, provoking

Strategy: Inform those who will be impacted by your actions

Emotional Theme: Anger/Peace

Wealth Theme: Start and leverage something for passive revenue

Challenges: Lack of sustainable energy, moves faster than others, accessing the right kind of support

Percentage of People Who Are Manifestors: 8 percent

Role: Initiate action from ideas and from their own inner creative flow

Famous Manifestors: Richard Burton, George W. Bush, Al Gore, Jack Nicholson, Vladimir Putin, Susan Sarandon

Manifestors are a minority—around 8 percent of all people. If you are a Manifestor, you have an Open Sacral Center and an active Channel that connects either the Will Center, the Emotional Solar Plexus, or the Root Center to the Throat Center (see Figure 23).

Manifestors are the only Type designed to initiate action. They get the ball rolling—they make things happen. All the other Types have to wait before they can take action.

With the sense of knowing the right timing, it's unnecessary for Manifestors to wait for outside confirmation before taking action. In spite of this ability to

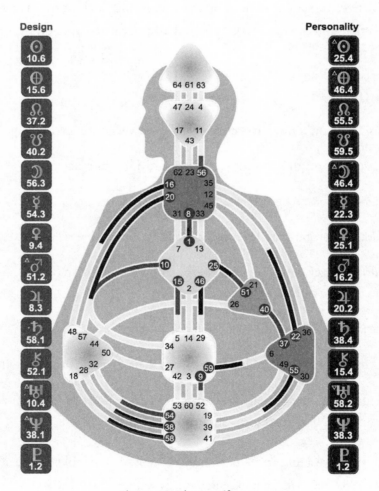

Figure 23: The Manifestor.

self-initiate, many Manifestors have their own personal way of interacting with the flow of life and wait for signs in their outer world to tell them that the timing is right to act.

Manifestors are powerful creative beings with an internal, nonverbal creative flow that moves quickly when the timing is correct. This creative flow is so fast that there often isn't time to put words to it. That means when a Manifestor intuitively senses that the timing is right, they can just get up and get to it.

A Manifestor's energy field carries with it the power to initiate others into action. When people are in a Manifestor's energy, they are often unconsciously poised, meaning they are ready to leap and get things going. Because of this frequency of energy, people pay attention to Manifestors, are always waiting to see what will happen next, and will often interrupt the creative flow.

This interruption can be very difficult and disruptive for a Manifestor's sense of flow. When you must stop that flow to find the words to explain to someone what you're doing or that you don't need help, it's often hard to find your creative flow in the same way again. When you don't understand how your energy works, it's easy to react with anger toward others, and other people can also become angry with you because they feel that you aren't involving them or are sometimes being inconsiderate of them when they don't know what you're doing.

As a way of dealing with a Manifestor's energy, others may want to help. This stems from their need to feel useful, but it's not the Manifestor's obligation to fulfill that need. If you are a Manifestor, you may find you are trying to keep others happy to avoid the anger or attempts to control you that you may have often experienced in your life. You may have developed elaborate strategies to secretly do what you want without interference. Not being up front and honest, as hard as it can be, uses up a lot of energy and can exhaust you whenever you feel like you have to deal with people. The truth is that you could be done with what you're doing in the time it can take to find the right words and try to explain to someone what you're doing. But you'll lose your speed if you don't stop and inform the people around you what you're going to do next.

If you're a Manifestor, the trick is learning to honor your inner creative flow and letting the people who will be impacted by your actions know what you're doing. Informing is not asking permission. You're not here to ask people for permission.

Learning to honor your creative flow, informing others, and not letting other people's discomfort interfere with your choices are often the greatest area of learning and growth for Manifestors.

Common Traps and Challenges

Working nine to five or more is difficult and unnatural for the Manifestor because they don't have sufficient sustainable energy for work. Manifestors don't usually make good team players and tend to want to do everything themselves. Delegating can be hard for them because they feel they'll be able to complete a task faster themselves. Finding the words for their creative flow slows them down and feels unnatural.

Manifestors have a unique energy that makes it easier for them to get things started. Sometimes, when you're a Manifestor, it's easy to lose your patience with other people who simply are not wired the way you are. It can also be difficult, once you get something started, to follow through with the energy to bring it to completion or to manage your creation on a day-to-day level. Remember, you're an initiator, not necessarily a doer.

Manifestors do not have sustainable life and work force energy, which is why most are not particularly good at seeing a project or fulfilling an idea to its end. Manifestors are not designed to finish the sustained implementation of ideas and projects. The follow-through and maintenance tasks are not in their Type. Theirs is a creative and initiating energy. They originate opportunities and move on to create the next.

Manifestors give the rest of us reasons to respond—like the cue ball on a pool table, bumping into the other balls and causing them to move.

Strategy

If you are a Manifestor, it's correct for you to start things but not necessarily implement the details or finish the projects. You must learn to delegate and/or move on when it feels correct to do so.

If you're feeling stuck or shut down, start initiating more in your life. It's okay to begin with small tasks and projects to rebuild that initiating muscle. After all, it may have been suppressed for most (or all) of your life. You'll feel much better when you are behaving the way you are designed to behave. And you'll have more energy.

Remember to inform people who may be impacted by your actions before you act. It takes courage to do this; it will take time for it to become a habit but will be absolutely worth it. Your relationships and even your health and wellness will improve because of it. It will also minimize the amount of anger and resistance that you experience from others.

Keep in mind that informing is *not* asking for permission, so don't be afraid of others saying no or trying to stop you. You can still do as intended, but it'll be wise to take others' views into consideration if you can—there's nothing wrong with a second opinion!

Recognize the impact you have on people around you. You have a very strong and powerful aura. Others will usually feel your presence when you enter a room. Some Manifestors are surprised to learn this about themselves, but the people around them know it to be true.

Trust what feels right—not just what your brain-based analysis tells you. Manage your energy and take breaks when needed. It's much easier to avoid burnout than to recover from it.

Manifestors can initiate action and opportunity without waiting. Manifestors are energy beings that possess tremendous initiating power, but they must use their power carefully or risk angering others.

Their purpose in life is to create action for a reaction. If a Manifestor decides to start a business, for example, all they have to do is pick the right timing and then just do it. All the other Types should wait before they can take action.

Although most of us think we would love to be Manifestors, being a Manifestor can have its own challenges. Many Manifestors have struggled to learn to use their power appropriately and may be conditioned to hide their power—or suppress it entirely.

Manifestors must learn how to channel their energy properly or they will face tremendous resistance in life. Properly channeled Manifestor energy often gives the other Types ideas for projects for responding.

Without informing, you will get resistance every step of the way. That's why many Manifestors (already starting in their childhood) resign after being punished repeatedly by parents, teachers, and others who don't understand the power of the Manifestor. When Manifestors give up their manifesting powers, they surrender to going through life just getting by. They may feel ignored or like they've been run over by a truck. The last thing they would want to do is to inform others. Everybody else is in their way all the time, so the idea of making it easier for others by informing seems unacceptable. Yet, it's the only way out of the circle of control and resistance.

Emotional Theme

The emotional theme of the Manifestor is anger. Anger often happens when people inadvertently slow you down, try to help you, or tell you that you can't do something. Not having the skills to manage your anger properly can sometimes be destructive.

Manifestors often struggle with knowing when enough is enough. If you're a Manifestor, it's important to gauge what you're doing and make sure you're not frying everyone else's energy, causing them to burn out. If you are, that doesn't mean that you should stop what you're doing, but be aware that sometimes this may trigger anger in others.

On an energy level you make quite the impression on others, but your aura doesn't communicate as much as the auras of other Types. Because of this, others are not sure how to accept you, which is why communication is so important. Inform those in your circle of influence, as this is how to release tension. By bringing others into the conversation, they may help you and put their energy into whatever it is that you have initiated. At that point, you will find what you've been seeking: completion of your creative inspiration.

Relationships

If you love a Manifestor, see that you don't take their anger personally; understand that it's part of their process.

Accept that they may not need you in the way you need them and that it's nothing against you. They are designed to act on their own, but they can engage and inspire people when in tune with those around them—particularly when keeping them informed of their dreams and plans.

Don't interrupt a Manifestor when they're in their groove of figuring things out and getting things done. They're not ignoring you—they are simply completely engaged in their own internal process. Keep them informed about your actions and make it easy for them to inform you without fear of recrimination or rejection.

Respect their privacy; don't ask or pry. They may not always be able to articulate what's going on in their mind.

Trust them in their role of initiating action and giving others things to which they may respond—that's what they're here to do.

Don't judge or criticize when they start then stop projects. Trying is often the only way a Manifestor can know if something is correct for them. Allow them their own consequences—they usually don't want to be helped unless they've asked for it. See Figure 24.

Figure 24: Loving a Manifestor.

Manifestor Children

One of the hardest things to do when you are a parent of a Manifestor is to let them go and allow them to discover their own inner creative flow. It's ironic that most parents of Manifestors want to hold them back. This isn't because you want to control or harm your child. It's just that the aura of a Manifestor sends the message that this is a child who follows a different set of rules, who isn't necessarily going to follow imposed rules, and who is often quite proficient and effective at taking care of themselves.

Here are a few things that Manifestor children need:

- The freedom to follow their creative input

- To be informed and to learn to inform

- Downtime and regular rest

- To learn when enough is enough

The natural response of parents is to want to hold tight, to keep this creative force from going out into the world and getting hurt, or to stop the child from taking big risks. The challenge for parents of Manifestors is learning to trust your child's inner creative instincts and wisdom while helping your child to grow as well as thrive.

Manifestor children need a lot of freedom to experiment and explore. They also need downtime to restore and nourish their energy. They need to be carefully informed about plans and what to expect so that they can flow along with the rest of the family.

Work

The design of Manifestors can very much affect relationships as well as work and life choices.

Manifestors can and do have jobs or businesses and raise families, but they may burn out around age fifty or before if they continue attempting to accomplish too much, especially if they're pushing themselves to keep up with the 70 percent of the population who have consistent Sacral energy.

Manifestors don't need people the way other Types need people, which affects how they operate within relationships. The biggest challenge—and a key piece of their Strategy for success in life—is *informing* those who are affected by their actions before acting.

More so than other Types, Manifestors don't like being told what to do. If they feel obligated to ask permission to do something or feel manipulated or repressed in any way, they may become overtly defiant and angry or turn those feelings inward, creating anxiety, depression, or even illness.

Health

For Manifestors to stay healthy, they need to be powerful. Repressed Manifestor energy doesn't go away; it ricochets inside in the body, either causing burnout or sometimes creating depression and anxiety.

If you have had a lifetime of using your power without informing others, if you have fought and struggled to keep people out of your way so that you can do what you feel like you need to do, then you may also experience burnout.

Most Manifestors burn out around the age of fifty if they haven't been using their energy properly. Burnout can come from not knowing when enough is enough, pushing without the balance of rest, trying to work in ways that are not in alignment with your energy, and denying your own power. If you're burned out, the number one priority in your life is healing from that. Often that means stopping everything in your life and catching up on the rest you need to restore and recharge.

Getting good, healthy sleep is of particular importance for Manifestors, which requires lying down before fatigue sets in. Reading, watching a movie, meditating—basically being in a horizontal position—releases the energy from the day and helps the body discharge any excess. If possible, Manifestors should try to sleep alone, out of range of other people's auras—or as far away from the energy of others as possible. If you can do this, you will feel the difference in the morning.

Wealth

Passive revenue streams or ways of making money via investments are important for Manifestors. If you are a young Manifestor, start saving early and invest your money.

Spiritual Theme

Manifestors have powerful auras and have an energetic impact on those around them. That impact can be positive and pull people in, or it can repel people.

They have a much easier time making things happen in the world than any of the other Types if they are living true to their Type. The Manifestor is tuned in to the flow of creation in the world. They are energetic messengers, designed to take actions that initiate a flow of divine inspiration on the planet.

If you're a Manifestor, you have a powerful role in changing the world. You may have, at various times in your life, wondered if you had a purpose or a reason for being here. The more connected you are to your own spiritual practice, the more aligned you will feel with the purpose and the greater service you will offer the world—in the way that's right for you.

Manifestor Life Purpose Statement: I serve the world by trusting my own inner creative flow and following through with action. My actions initiate new ideas and possibilities and change the world.

Affirmations

I am a powerful creative force. I trust my own inner sense of timing to take action on my creative intentions. I follow my creative flow and inform those who may be impacted by my actions so that they can support me and clear the path for me to do what I need to do. I recognize my value and know that when I follow my creative flow, I am not only bringing something new into the world, I am initiating others into new possibilities. I value the unique role that only I can play. I honor my power and commit myself to nurturing my energy so that I can act with great power when the timing is correct. I am a transformational force, and my actions change the world.

Manifestor Examples

I was working in a restaurant. It was a great place, very artsy, creative, and liberal. New art every month. I had worked there part-time for a year. The place was great, but the waitstaff and head waiter were pretty low vibration and not creative or inspired, like they did not want to be there. I was thinking of quitting, because I just did not connect with anyone there and I was bummed because I loved the restaurant.

I was at home going off to sleep when I suddenly thought, "I am going to go in there tomorrow and uplift the energy and just have fun even if no one else is. There is supposed to be a creative alive energy in this place."

So, the next day I went in with a high vibe and was joking with the customers and having fun. Every time I went in after, I was joyful and playful. Over the course of the next few weeks, the other waitstaff left to go on to new things. Then the new waitstaff came in and they were really lovely and creative and happy to be there. The whole vibe changed into this awesome place. More customers came in, and it became a totally happening and abundant place.

Then the head waiter left also, and they made me head waitress. The place just totally transformed into a whole new restaurant, full of joy and laughter.

It seems I initiated the restaurant into a whole new vibration from what I decided that night before going off to sleep. The creative alignment that flowed thereafter was truly amazing.

This happened before I knew I was a Manifestor. It was one of the first times I saw how much my energy, or the creative intelligence through me, could impact the field, especially through my feeling tone. Like if I held a certain vibration, I could create a ripple effect.

—Joanne

When I wanted to travel across the country to interview courageous women for my book, I shared the idea with my team at the lifestyle brand I worked at. They introduced me to some great women, who introduced me to more great women. I had the idea to live in a van for thirty days to do it, and the perfect van became available at a local dealership. I initiated a friend to convert it, and in two days I found a photographer to come with me who I met in a coffee shop for forty-five minutes! I was able to raise over ten thousand dollars on a Kickstarter campaign to help with the costs, and voilà! A book was born.

—Tara

The Pure Generator and the Manifesting Generator

There are two kinds of Generators: Pure Generators (see Figure 25) and Manifesting Generators (see Figure 27). About 70 percent of us are Generators. Pure and Manifesting Generators have Defined Sacral Centers that allow them the gift to create the work of the world.

The Pure Generator

Focus: Respond, right work, family, mastery, here to build

Strategy: Respond, then act

Emotional Theme: Frustration

Wealth Theme: Mastery over time

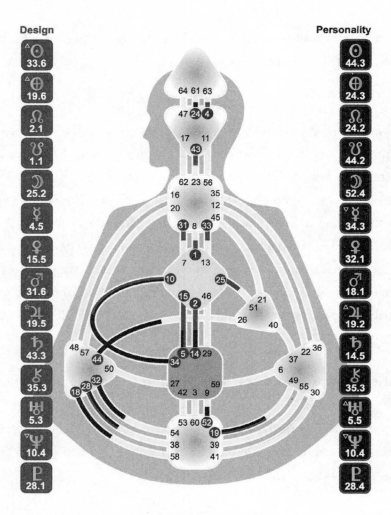

Figure 25: The Pure Generator.

Challenges: Finding right work, frustration and quitting, patience and waiting, trusting their inner response

Percentage of People Who Are Pure Generators: 35 percent

Role: To do the work of the world and to find mastery in their work

Famous Pure Generators: Deepak Chopra, Bill Clinton, James Dean, Albert Einstein, Greta Garbo, Jay-Z, Carl Jung, Kim Kardashian, the Dalai Lama, Timothy Leary, John Lennon, Madonna, Elvis Presley, Meg Ryan, Meryl Streep, Margaret Thatcher, Oprah Winfrey

Generators play the part of patient seekers who become fully activated in their life purpose when they learn to respond to what the world brings them, instead of trying to figure out with their minds what they should be doing. Generators have the potential to be masters of what they respond to, to do and to create.

Generators know they hold this energy. If you're a Generator, you often feel frustrated because you can sense that you're here to do something that fulfills your full potential. As a Generator, you're trained by the world to use your thinking and the power of your mind to set your path to mastery. The truth for Generators is that the path is revealed to you by the world outside of yourself; it takes faith and the understanding of how to connect with that path correctly to align yourself with your destiny and the ultimate fulfillment of your potential.

In other words, if you're a Generator, you can't simply follow your ideas. You must wait for confirmation outside of yourself that these two things are true:

- Your idea is actually the right idea for you

- The timing is right to take action on your idea

Common Traps and Challenges

Most Generators have been taught to bypass their inner wisdom and to adopt a "just do it" attitude about the things they think they should be doing. Generators may find it difficult to refrain from "just doing it" because it requires ignoring old programming and old ideas about hard work, success, and money. It can feel scary or irresponsible to follow your gut and forgo the programming of your mind.

Because Generators are energy beings, they have the energy to work, even at jobs they hate. Sadly, many Generators do this for their entire lives. When a Generator is simply working, but not working at a job they respond to, they fail to tap into the full expression of their potential and the vital life force energy that turns on when they respond to doing the work that feels right. When a Generator responds hastily, frustration and burnout eventually ensue. It's not until Generators are patient, hold off on pursuing what they think they should be doing, and let their life path unfold in front of them that the energy appears. In essence, it's like waiting for a sign or signal that the timing must be right before acting.

When a Generator waits, they create a magical force that attracts everyone—an energy that will continue to grow until a true purpose appears. Every Generator has a fear that if they do nothing, then no one will ask them anything. But every Generator who has the courage to wait soon sees that fear is unfounded. When a Generator waits and steps into their full purpose and potential, they wake up to a vitality and a joy that they've been waiting for their whole lives.

Strategy

The Generator Strategy is to wait to respond. This is a simple although often confusing aspect for the Generator. "Wait to respond" simply means that even if you have an incredibly inspiring insight, thought, or idea, you need to wait for confirmation in your outer world before you take action.

Confirmation in your outside world can be someone saying something to you, a sign from the Universe, or some kind of physical initiation that comes from outside your mind. Once you get the sign or something you know you should respond to, you can then act on the inspirations that feel good and right.

As a Generator, in order to find your path, you have to learn how to use your energy correctly. Generators are the only Type who have a Defined Sacral Motor. The Sacral Motor is the spirit of direction-giving: it's a nonverbal, gut-level vibration that tells you what feels right and what doesn't.

You may experience the Sacral response as a gut feeling, and you can connect with it even more deeply when you express that feeling with a nonverbal sound such as *uh-huh* for yes and *un-uhn* for no. This Sacral sound is the sound of your inner intuition, the vibrational alignment with your correct direction in life. It is that direction that will take you to the next step in the unfolding of your mastery. The Sacral is truth; it cannot lie.

Most Generators naturally make these sounds but are often taught that they are rude or to "use your words instead." When you watch Generator children, you'll notice that they are grunting, humming, sound-based beings.

The Sacral Center is a spirit of sustainable energy. All the motors in the Human Design System, except for the Sacral, have wavelike, inconsistent qualities; but the Sacral Center keeps going and going. It provides energy for work and the life force. It's about providing the resources and education and taking care of the children, family, tribe, and community. It's about work in every way and doing it all sustainably.

Generators have two primary focuses in life—work and family—and they will feel most fulfilled when they are pursuing either or both of these.

For Generators, life is about response. Instead of chasing after an imitation life, Generators must be patient and allow an authentic life to appear. The goal of a Generator is to discover, pursue, and dedicate their life to what they love.

Emotional Theme

The Sacral sounds turn on the Sacral Motor. This sound-based gut feeling, the spirit of the truth, is unique to Generators. You must ask questions of yourself and monitor your gut response with the *uh-huh* and *un-unh* answers. When you aren't responding and instead are trying to force things into creation, you will most likely experience frustration.

The Sacral Center is a tremendous energy generator that provides all energy. Sacral energy is enough to do all things when you follow that gut pulse. Generators who don't respond to the energy end up deeply frustrated. It's imperative to remain patient and recognize the presence of the energy when it appears. The power of the Defined Sacral Center will lead the way to one's true life purpose. Trust your inner response. The Sacral Center provides Generators with a virtually inexhaustible spirit of energy.

Generators can find themselves confined to work they hate, feeling the drudgery of routine without joy, lost in unproductive labor, sensing there is something missing, knowing they may have made a mistake—and not knowing how to get out of it unless they quit. Ultimately, they will burn out or live life at a level of compromise, which will create frustration or despair.

There is a second spirit of natural frustration for the Generator, too. Generators have a stair-step learning curve. Once a Generator responds to a new opportunity, there will be a surge in mastery. It feels good to be doing or learning something new, and Generators learn quickly. But eventually, all Generators hit a plateau.

Plateauing is normal for Generators, and it is a phase of learning, energy integration, and growth. The plateau can be dangerous for the Generator who doesn't understand their unique energy. Many Generators tend to quit when they are on the plateau, failing to recognize that the plateau is simply a normal part of the Generator process.

Once you understand that it is crucial to wait for the next thing to respond to when you are on the plateau, you are present and ready when the next step to your growth and mastery appears. Frustration is simply a sign that you are getting ready for something new. But if you quit instead of wait, as many Generators do, you may miss the next true opportunity. Instead, you spend a lifetime of repetitious starting and quitting, never getting to be masterful at what you are really created to do.

Relationships

Trust your relationship with a Generator. Allow the Generator time to wait for things that will prompt a response. The Generator also needs the freedom to honor and follow their responses—even if their responses don't appear to be logical.

The most respectful—and helpful—way that you can interact with a Generator is to ask them yes/no questions. This gives them a clear opportunity for their Sacral Center to respond and give them guidance.

Don't take their frustration/anger/impatience personally. Recognize that it's part of their process, and when you support them in being true to their Generator nature, you'll help them minimize all the things that are distractions to them and confusing to you. Understand that it is correct for them to wait for their inner guidance before they take action.

Once this energy difference in your relationship is truly understood and respected, you'll both be happier (see Figure 26). Most of all, enjoy the ride!

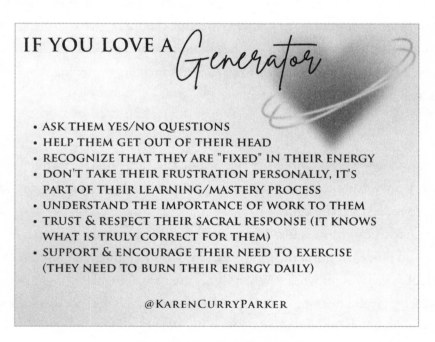

IF YOU LOVE A *Generator*

- ASK THEM YES/NO QUESTIONS
- HELP THEM GET OUT OF THEIR HEAD
- RECOGNIZE THAT THEY ARE "FIXED" IN THEIR ENERGY
- DON'T TAKE THEIR FRUSTRATION PERSONALLY, IT'S PART OF THEIR LEARNING/MASTERY PROCESS
- UNDERSTAND THE IMPORTANCE OF WORK TO THEM
- TRUST & RESPECT THEIR SACRAL RESPONSE (IT KNOWS WHAT IS TRULY CORRECT FOR THEM)
- SUPPORT & ENCOURAGE THEIR NEED TO EXERCISE (THEY NEED TO BURN THEIR ENERGY DAILY)

@KARENCURRYPARKER

Figure 26: Loving a Generator.

Pure Generator Children

Generator children need to learn about their own inner compass and their Sacral energy. It is vital for Generator children to learn to respond. Yes/No question games that help them respond with the Sacral sounds are fun, enlivening, and vital to helping Generator children stay connected to their own inner truth. They need to:

- Explore and engage in activities

- Learn in a self-paced environment

- Engage in daily exercise and physical activity

- Learn to trust their Sacral response by being allowed to respond appropriately

Generator children need to move and groove. They need a lot of physical activity to wear them out and promote good sleep every day. Too much time sitting and a lack of movement can cause Generator children to have challenges with sleep and even their health. Turn off the computers, don't overdo the homework and after-school activities, and help your Generator child get moving. Your whole family will benefit!

Work

Generators are the great workers of the world. They are often performing relentless work they hate, tolerating a lifetime of labor while waiting for the Sacral energy to reveal their life's goal.

The one true purpose is for Generators to be patient, to trust their tremendous energy and power to fulfill their purpose of not only finding, but also becoming masterful at their "right work." When Generators are doing their "right work"—the work that feels satisfying and juicy—then they not only feel good, but they are adding to the wholeness and abundance of the world.

Satisfaction is a key word for Generators; it's all about tapping into their Sacral energies that open the door to the satisfaction of work and family. Their Sacral response will take them to where they can experience the greatest satisfaction, vitality, and joy.

Health

Your brain will often work hard to figure out the right answers, but that is not where you want to be making your decisions and choices. That's what your Sacral responses are intended to do. Generators who have not tuned in to their Sacral Motor for a lifetime are vulnerable to burnout. Not being true to your energy and trying to do something that doesn't satisfy you can make you exhausted.

Here are some ways that Generators can lose energy or burn out:

- Not loving their work or environment

- Choosing a sedentary lifestyle

- Not following their Sacral guidance

- Overexerting themselves and not recharging their energy

- Feeling frustrated and impatient when results aren't quickly realized

Generators have their own inner guidance system—the Sacral Center—that can tell them what they need to do for health and wellness. They need to respond to what's healthy. It must feel right and aligned with their Sacral to commit to a health and wellness routine.

As energy beings, Generators need a lot of movement and exercise to burn off excess energy. Generators who are struggling with insomnia or poor-quality sleep can benefit from more physical activity.

Wealth

The wealth theme of the Generator is to become masterful at whatever makes them respond. But, for Generators, recognizing when to respond and when to remain dormant is their greatest challenge.

Most Generators become frustrated when they hit their plateau of inertia, and many quit before they surge in mastery; this denies them the blessing and opportunity of experiencing whatever it is they are here to build in the world. To align with true abundance, the Generators must learn to wait and manage their frustration in healthy and dynamic ways to be ready to master life's purpose.

Generator Types can work—even work hard, to make money provided that the work they are doing is something to which they have responded positively with their Sacral Motors. The more they love their work and their masterful contribution, the easier it becomes for them to create and maintain wealth. Frustrated and burned-out Generators can often overspend their funds as a way of overcompensating for their frustration.

Patience and passion are the keys to building true wealth for a Generator.

Spiritual Theme

A Generator will wait to respond in a world that's been taught to pursue arbitrary opportunities. By this nature, it's imperative that Generators be patient and wait to see what the Universe delivers to them. Only then, when the right thing shows up—the thing that feels right—do Generators follow that feeling, respond, and take right action.

The goal of the Generator is to achieve mastery. Generators cannot achieve mastery if they're leaping into things that don't feel right because they are afraid to trust in the natural unfolding of their life and the abundance of the Universe.

It is the Generator's job to take inspiration and give it form through creative work. The Generators build the manifested form of Cosmic Order, and when they follow their Sacral impulses, they are led to their right place and their right destiny in the world.

The spiritual challenge of the Generator is to trust the unfolding of the divine order and their place in it by trusting the inner wisdom of their Sacral impulse.

Generator Life Purpose Statement: I serve the world by finding and doing the work that brings me deep satisfaction. My work transforms ideas into reality. I am a builder of the world.

Affirmations

My life gives me an arena within which to explore myself and who I am. I let my inner alignment with my truth—and what feels good and right—guide me and reveal to me the next right step. I strengthen my self-trust and courage so that I can confidently follow my path. I use the power of my mind to inspire me and allow for the gentle unfolding of my life path. I trust in the cycles of growth in my life, knowing that my destiny is to be the fulfillment of who I am. I listen to the signal that frustration gives me, knowing that my frustration is informing me that change is coming.

Pure Generator Examples

Four years ago, after a diagnosis that an old whiplash injury to my neck had caught up with me, I decided to grieve everything I wasn't going to be able to do anymore (like trampoline jumping, roller-coaster rides, etc.).

In responding, by surrendering to the reality of my body's physical state, I initiated, much to my delight, the healing energy of what is possible when honoring endings. I let go of all "I can't do's" and began seeing all "I can do's" instead, freeing up bandwidth.

I unstuck myself from limiting beliefs and conditioning and opened up to the potential and possibilities of vibrant health and vitality, which I am enjoying today, free of drugs, pain, and brain fog.

—Marina

The Manifesting Generator

Focus: Shortcuts to mastery, respond, right work, family, here to build

Strategy: Respond, then envision, inform, then act

Emotional Theme: Frustration and anger

Wealth Theme: Mastery over time

Challenges: Finding right work, frustration and quitting, patience and waiting, trusting their inner response (Sacral)

Percentage of People Who Are Manifesting Generators: 35 percent

Role: To do the work of the world and to find mastery in their work

Famous Manifesting Generators: Marie Antoinette, Frederic Chopin, Hillary Clinton, Marie Curie, Clint Eastwood, Sigmund Freud, Mahatma Gandhi, Steffi Graf, Mikhail Gorbachev, Jimi Hendrix, Pope John Paul II, Janis Joplin, Martin Luther King Jr., Nicki Minaj, Friedrich Nietzsche, Richard Nixon, Jacqueline Onassis, Yoko Ono, Prince, Vincent van Gogh, Malala Yousafzai

Note: If you are a Manifesting Generator, you are a hybrid of the Manifestor and the Generator. Please read the Manifestor section along with the Generator section to get more insights into how you operate.

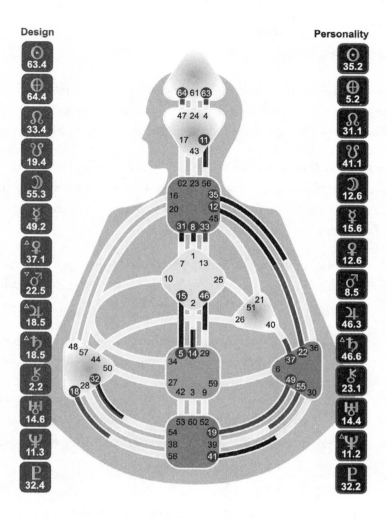

Figure 27: The Manifesting Generator.

Manifesting Generators have a deep inner awareness about what's right for them, as they wait for a sign or a signal that the timing is right to act. A strong intuition turned on by gut-level pulses will simultaneously place Manifesting Generators in the right place, doing the right work, and having the right impact.

Common Traps and Challenges

What makes a Manifesting Generator?

- A Defined Sacral Center, the most powerful motor in the body, focuses work and life force energy. This means Manifesting Generators have the ability to multitask work and family.

- A motorized energy connects through a Channel to the throat. This means Manifesting Generators can initiate conversations, although they still need to act like Generators in other areas of their lives. (They need to wait to respond.)

- Finding the right work and right partner in life is important; and finding the fastest way to accomplish this is the way a Manifesting Generator will approach these topics.

- Patience is extremely important in waiting to respond with Sacral energy. Informing everyone in your "impact field" of your plans before you act needs to be top of mind.

Manifesting Generators determine the fastest way to complete tasks, often skipping steps in the process while getting things done. If they find those skipped steps to be important, they will eventually complete them.

Manifesting Generators are the busiest Type. They are intense multitaskers, filled with enormous bursts of energy who feel nothing seems to move fast enough. When fatigue comes, they will take the time to recharge, only to start all over again.

Strategy

Manifesting Generators have two primary focuses in life: work and family.

Manifesting Generators are often serial entrepreneurs. They need and love to do more than one thing at a time—and this is considered normal and healthy for them. They often speed through creating anything and everything they consider. They do not have to complete these projects but instead need to follow the flow of the projects that feel good as they are unfolding in a satisfying way.

This process of trying many things simultaneously often causes others to judge the Manifesting Generator for overcommitting or lack of focus, but this is actually an important part of the creative process of the Manifesting Generator. They need to be free to try many things at once.

Manifesting Generators are designed to discover the shortcut—the fastest, easiest way to get things done.

Once they begin a project, Manifesting Generators will have the best results when including family, team, staff, or peers, as they, too, will be affected by the actions. However, Manifesting Generators (much like the Manifestor) have to inform these groups about the actions prior to following through.

Manifesting Generators (and Pure Generators) recognize that the most important thing in life is finding the right work. If a Manifesting Generator isn't working on something they love, burnout occurs; if satisfaction isn't found, frustration and unhappiness take hold. In contrast, when they realize their true work, the Sacral Center provides them a virtually inexhaustible spirit of energy.

Manifesting Generators respond quite quickly to situations because of the motor to the Throat, so it's difficult to tell the difference between responding and initiating. Once a response is made, the Manifesting Generator should stop and envision their next decision. They will do well if ideas are imagined first for a visualized outcome before actually doing them. However, they must still wait before taking action.

Emotional Theme

Manifesting Generators experience deep frustration by initiating things. Of course, waiting can feel very challenging. It may feel unnatural, particularly in our culture, as we are told to just get out there and do it. Make something happen. If you're a

Manifesting Generator, experiment with waiting—even if it's just a few days. See what happens!

When Manifesting Generators wait, things always come to them at the right time and in the right way. Their energy field communicates to the world that they need something that will enable them to respond to it. Manifesting Generators have similar energy characteristics as Manifestors, though they tend to respond more quickly to situations than a Pure Generator.

It may seem that Manifesting Generators continually change their minds. For them, the need to internally check responses by trial and error confirms (or not) if what they've started is still good for them. In essence, it's like waiting for a sign or a signal that the timing is right before taking action. Manifesting Generators have a gut instinct that, when followed correctly, always puts them in the right place at the right time.

A Manifesting Generator is uniquely capable of getting more accomplished than most, and for a longer time period. For those who don't respond, they run the risk of being very busy accomplishing nothing.

The emotional themes of the Manifesting Generator are anger (from the Manifesting part) and frustration (from the Generator part). Manifesting Generators must also inform like Manifestors to stabilize the energy around them. They can move so quickly that informing feels like it is slowing them down, but informing will decrease the resistance they get from others.

Like Pure Generators, Manifesting Generators tend to sit on plateaus before they have breakthroughs. It's common for Manifesting Generators to quit and go in a different direction right before a breakthrough. Part of this is attributable to finding work they love. If they don't love their work, it's hard to get it done. If you're feeling stuck and you're a Manifesting Generator, it might be good to consider if you really love what you're doing for work. As a Manifesting Generator, your passion is the most profitable part of your business. No passion = no profit.

Sometimes, Manifesting Generators get out of balance. They love their work so much that they can forget to come up for air. Manifesting Generators move very quickly, and like Manifestors they often have a hard time with being team players. Delegating and letting go can be challenging; they often need help triaging their time as well as energy and making sure they're not doing everything just because they can.

Relationships

Manifesting Generators who use their inherent energy correctly and follow the inner guidance of their Sacral response are a dynamic and powerful force. They benefit the world in work and relationships—and they are magnificent to watch in action.

Manifesting Generators can be committed and steady partners in the right relationships. However, when they're in a groove, they prefer to be left alone—and this can be a problem for some relationships! Sometimes when Manifesting Generators are in partnership, they can steamroll their partner and peers by virtue of their speed as well as focus on getting the job done.

In addition, all Manifesting Generators will occasionally forget to inform their partners about projects, leaving them confused, angry, or stressed about what might be going on in the relationship. The outer frenetic appearance of the Manifesting Generator creativity can sometimes leave loved ones feeling overwhelmed by their energy. Informing can help soften the intensity, but the creative spark combined with the sustainability of the Sacral energy can feel like it's too much at various times.

As a Manifesting Generator, if you're not waiting for life to come to you and responding to it, you won't know what is truly right and worth your considerable energy and competence. Have you been rushing off responses and finding yourself scattered in a bunch of different directions? The problem with this approach is that it's just not correct for you. Hence, you will experience many wrong directions, accompanied by frustration, anger, and impatience.

Sadly, closest relationships often bear the brunt of those types of reactions. When you wait and follow your inner guidance, you'll have less frustration spilling onto others. Recognizing that the frustration and anger are energy will help minimize the negative impact on others. However, frustration is part of your personal learning curve, so you won't be avoiding it entirely. It takes courage to wait for, trust, and follow your Sacral response—but everything in your life (including relationships) will benefit when you do.

You'll be more effective in your relationships when you work at being as respectful of others as you can, watch out for power struggles, and learn to compromise. Also, remember to inform others of your plans before you take action. Don't worry about skipping steps, moving fast, and multitasking—you are designed for these!

Be physically active during the day so that you are tired and sleep well at night. You'll wake up each morning with another full tank of gas to be used all over again. (This is especially true for Manifesting Generator children: Many are incorrectly diagnosed with ADD or ADHD.)

If you are not a Manifesting Generator but are in a relationship with one (see Figure 28), follow these guidelines:

- Accept that they move fast and may leave you behind at times. Don't try to keep up—you will wear down and burn out. Once this energy difference in your relationship is truly understood and respected, you'll both be happier.

- Understand that a Manifesting Generator should wait for their inner guidance before they act. Grant them the freedom to honor and follow their responses—even if their responses appear to not be logical.

IF YOU LOVE A *Manifesting Generator*

- ASK THEM YES/NO QUESTIONS
- DON'T TELL THEM WHAT TO DO
- DON'T INTERRUPT THEIR FLOW
- GIVE THEM FREEDOM TO GO AT THEIR OWN SPEED & DON'T TRY TO KEEP UP
- DON'T TRY TO MAKE THEM DO ONE THING AT A TIME, IT'S CORRECT FOR THEM TO MULTITASK & SKIP STEPS
- JUST LIKE THEY INFORM YOU, THEY ALSO NEED TO BE INFORMED
- DON'T TAKE THEIR FRUSTRATION/ANGER/IMPATIENCE PERSONALLY, IT'S PART OF THEIR LEARNING/MASTERY PROCESS
- TRUST & RESPECT THEIR SACRAL RESPONSE (IT KNOWS WHAT IS TRULY CORRECT FOR THEM)
- SUPPORT & ENCOURAGE THEIR NEED TO EXERCISE (THEY NEED TO BURN THEIR ENERGY DAILY)

@KarenCurryParker

Figure 28: Loving a Manifesting Generator.

- The most respectful and helpful way that you can interact with a Manifesting Generator is to ask them yes/no questions. This allows them a clear opportunity for their Sacral Center to respond and give them guidance.

- Don't take a Manifesting Generator's frustration/anger/impatience personally. Recognize that it's part of their process, and when you support them in being true to their nature, you'll help them minimize all of that.

Manifesting Generator Children

Just like the Generator child, the Manifesting Generator child needs to be given yes/no options, such as: "Do you want to wear your green shirt? Or do you like the blue shirt better?"

The more you allow Manifesting Generator children the freedom to choose, the more they stay connected with their inner authority and their inner compass that takes them to the right place and opportunities in life. A Manifesting Generator child needs:

- To explore and engage in activities that spark their interest and passion

- To learn in a self-paced environment

- To engage in plenty of exercise and physical activity daily

- To rest or go to bed when they are tired and not at a set time

- To be asked, "Do you want to do this?" "Does this feel good to you?" "Is this good for you at this time?" "Is it better for you to do this later?" and "I have a suggestion; do you want to hear it?"

Manifesting Generators may seem to start things and not finish them. While you want to encourage children to work toward mastering a skill set or an experience, it's also important for your Manifesting Generator to be allowed to try things and see how they feel before they commit to doing them.

Manifesting Generators often have a low tolerance for frustration and can seem to skip from thing to thing. It's important that you help them learn to connect with their Sacral sounds and stay tuned to the correct choices. Make sure that they don't quit unless they respond to quitting. Teach them ways to manage their overwhelming sensation and frustration; give them responsibility for figuring out how to be more masterful. (As a parent, sometimes it feels easier just to take over for your child or resolve the frustrating circumstances. If you do this, you rob your Manifesting Generator of important learning experiences.)

Work

The Manifesting Generator brain will often work hard to figure out the right answers, but that is not where you want to be making your decisions and choices. That's where your Sacral responses are purposeful. Manifesting Generators have to wait for something they can respond to before leaping into action. This is like waiting for a sign or a signal that the timing is right before acting.

Manifesting Generators have a deep inner awareness that pulses on or off. Following these strong gut-level pulses puts the Manifesting Generator in the right place, doing the right work, and having the right impact. In addition, Manifesting Generators have a unique ability to multitask. A Manifesting Generator is uniquely capable of getting more things done than most and for a long time.

Compared to the Pure Generator who has a much more deliberate process, if the two Types begin a job at the same time, it will appear the Manifesting Generator is faster and learns more quickly. However, six months later the Generator will have caught up, and they will both be at the same level of mastery.

Health

Manifesting Generators have sustainable life force and work force energy for doing. Like Generators, they are designed to start with a full tank every morning to be used before they go to bed. They are also designed to be fast processors (the fastest of the five Types), have a lot going on, and be good multitaskers. They may skip steps in their haste to get things done, but that's actually correct for them.

Although their energy is fast and sustainable, it is not inexhaustible even though they often think they are inexhaustible. Here are some ways that Manifesting Generators can lose energy or burn out:

- Not loving their work or environment

- Having a sedentary lifestyle

- Not following their Sacral guidance

- Overexerting themselves and not recharging their energy

- Feeling frustrated, angry, and impatient when results aren't forthcoming

Wealth

Just like the Generator who has a goal of achieving mastery, the Manifesting Generator cannot achieve mastery if they're leaping from thing to thing out of frustration.

The Sacral response is the Manifesting Generator's truth; it cannot lie and is turned on by two sounds: *uh-huh* and *un-unh*. When these sounds are emitted, the Sacral response can find its truth. The Sacral is far away from the head. So, when operating out of the rudimentary life force energy, if a Manifesting Generator finds themselves having to stop to use words, this means their energy is far away from their Sacral.

Your Sacral is your compass for life. It guides you on where you need to go, when you need to do something, and what needs to be accomplished. It's life force energy. That's your truth. When you focus on mastering these concepts, wealth follows.

Spiritual Theme

The spiritual role of the Manifesting Generator is to shorten the amount of time from thought form to creation. Manifesting Generators are here to remind us that creation can happen instantaneously if we remove our limitations and stay aligned with the unfolding of the divine plan.

Manifesting Generators have their own unique way of bending and using time. Watch the Manifesting Generators in your life, and you'll discover new ways to use time and flow.

Manifesting Generator Life Purpose: I serve the world by finding and doing the work that brings me deep satisfaction. Through my experimentation and exploration, I find the fastest, most effective way to transform ideas into reality. I am a builder of the world.

Affirmations

I move faster than most people. My speed and my ability to create many things simultaneously give me a unique perspective on how to get things done on the planet. Because I have a lot of energy, I need a lot of movement to stay healthy and strong. It's healthy for me to multitask, as I need to do more than one thing at a time to move my energy. Not everything I do will create the result that I'm envisioning. The purpose of multitasking is to burn off the extra energy that I carry. The things that are mine to complete and bring to the world will align with my inner sense of timing married with action. I am careful to let the people around me know what I'm doing so that they can stand back and let me create at my own speed.

Manifesting Generator Examples

When I first started learning Human Design in 1999, my first impulse was to teach a class about it. I booked a hotel conference room, placed flyers all over my community, posted an ad in the local newspaper, and eagerly prepared to welcome students to my class the night it was scheduled. Literally no one showed up, however, and it became abundantly clear to me that I was not responding when I initiated my idea to teach a class.

Three weeks later, I was talking to a friend and she suggested that I teach a class about Human Design. It felt as if a resonant bell was going off inside my body. I decided to conduct an experiment: I'd literally duplicate everything that I had done to lead the class I'd dreamed of three weeks earlier. I rented the same hotel room, remade the flyers with the new date, and resubmitted the press release to the newspaper. I had thirty-two people show up and made more money teaching a class than I'd ever made in my life up until that point. The only difference? I *initiated* one, which bombed, and I *responded* to one, which was a resounding success.

The Projector

Focus: Guidance, wisdom, intuitive, sensitive, sharing

Strategy: Wait to be invited

Emotional Theme: Bitterness

Wealth Theme: Self-mastery upon receiving invitation

Challenges: Waiting to receive the right invitation, giving away intellectual property

Percentage of People Who Are Projectors: 21 percent

Role: Manage, guide, and direct others

Famous Projectors: Woody Allen, Lance Armstrong, Chris Brown, Fidel Castro, Leonardo da Vinci, Queen Elizabeth II, Hugh Hefner, Mick Jagger, James Joyce, John F. Kennedy, Abraham Lincoln, Shirley MacLaine, Nelson Mandela, Karl Marx, Marilyn Monroe, Barack Obama, Osho, Brad Pitt, Ringo Starr, Barbra Streisand, Taylor Swift, Elizabeth Taylor, Kanye West

If you are a Projector, you are not here to work; you are here to know others, to recognize them, and to direct and guide them. But that can only happen if you are (1) recognized, and (2) invited to do so.

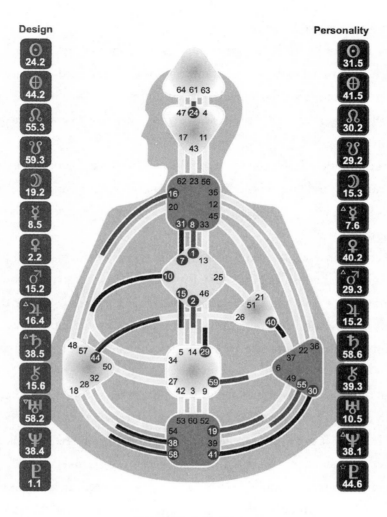

Design

☉ 24.2	
⊕ 44.2	
☊ 55.3	
☋ 59.3	
☽ 19.2	
☿ 8.5	
♀ 2.2	
♂ 15.2	
♃ 16.4	
♄ 38.5	
⚷ 15.6	
♅ 58.2	
♆ 38.4	
♇ 1.1	

Personality

☉ 31.5	
⊕ 41.5	
☊ 30.2	
☋ 29.2	
☽ 15.3	
☿ 7.6	
♀ 40.2	
♂ 29.3	
♃ 15.2	
♄ 58.6	
⚷ 39.3	
♅ 10.5	
♆ 38.1	
♇ 44.6	

Figure 29: A Projector.

Projectors can become the natural managers and leaders of the world. Projectors do not carry energy in their own personal field but absorb the energies of others and manage it. Projectors must wait to be recognized and invited into the major events in life such as love relationships, careers, and right place.

Common Traps and Challenges

The biggest challenge for Projectors is energy. Projectors don't have a lot of sustainable energy for working in the traditional way. They need to structure their business to allow for significant cycles of rest and restoration. Because hard work doesn't serve the Projector's purpose, learning how to leverage knowledge is important.

Projectors have a deep need for recognition. They often compromise their values for being seen and recognized. To many Projectors, being seen and recognized, even if it's for the wrong reasons, feels better than waiting for people to notice the value that they carry.

Projectors must value themselves enough to ensure they are paid for their ideas, insights, and consulting. It's easy for the Projector to give their intellectual property away for free, and some struggle with being heard or having their ideas stolen. It's counterintuitive, but learning to wait until someone asks is often the most profitable strategy for the Projector. It makes for an interesting way to do business and life.

When things don't go as planned or recognition feels slow in coming, the Projector can experience bitterness. Managing the bitterness is crucial, because if it's not kept in check it can repel people instead of attracting them. This takes a lot of self-mastery, patience, and trust in the abundance of the Universe.

If an invitation feels good for a Projector and is accepted, an enormous amount of energy and power is channeled into that situation, which may be used to manage others and all the world. The challenge for the Projector is to trust that the right invitations will come and to wait for those invitations. Sometimes, Projectors will wait months or even years for the right invitation. To influence the speed at which Projectors can receive invitations, they need two things: (1) the energy to implement the invitation, and (2) the self-worth to wait for an invitation that is truly honoring of their gifts and talents.

Compromising on these two factors can lead to burnout and bitterness.

Projectors, for all their wisdom, can have a frustrating and debilitating life if they try to push themselves to initiate action. A Projector simply does not have the energy to "just do it." If they try to initiate like a Manifestor or work steadily like a Generator, they will burn themselves out very quickly.

They are not here to work steadily like the Generator Types, and as a result Projectors may face a lot of judgment from others. They may be perceived as lazy, when in fact it is literally unhealthy for these Types to initiate any kind of action or to work at the wrong kind of jobs on a steady basis. They usually can't sustain the energy flow on their own.

Projectors are here to deeply understand others, and they can be powerful resources if they are recognized and used properly. A Projector can, simply by watching another energy Type, intuitively know how that other person can maximize their energy and their potential. This makes them natural coaches and mentors. Projectors are here to be recognized and invited by others.

Strategy

If you're a Projector, your Strategy is to wait for an invitation to the important areas of life. If your Authority says yes, then you can really share your gifts and guidance. To be invited means that you are seen and recognized for your values. If you don't wait for an invitation or the energy of invitation, you'll meet resistance.

Through your Open Centers, you take others in deeply. Your aura focuses on the very core of their being, and you clearly see who they are. But if you try to guide others without being invited to do so, you'll meet resistance or feel that no one really sees you. Out of that comes a deep feeling of bitterness, often mixed with exhaustion.

Projectors fear that they will not be invited. However, following the Strategy of waiting for the invitation changes the aura's frequency. The more in tune a Projector is with their design, the more invitations they will get. This will in turn bring great success. Once invited, there's no need to wait for any more offers. Just follow your Authority in doing what you do and don't initiate.

The invitation, the correct entry into anything, is the key. The feeling of being recognized, appreciated, heard, and seen—is it there? Great. If not, you may stop talking in midsentence and save yourself one more disappointment of not being understood.

A Projector's Openness can be energetically exhausting, so it is important they have their own space to relax. With an Undefined Sacral, they benefit from going to bed as soon as they begin to feel tired, and ideally they would sleep alone.

While the natural role and instinct of the Projector is to manage, guide, and direct others, the Projector can only do so effectively when others want to be managed, guided, and directed. Projectors are the eternal students of humanity and system masters. However, most people don't like to be given advice or told what to do if they haven't first asked for that advice or guidance. Projectors who are not using their energy—and their inherent wisdom—correctly are often perceived as pushy, bossy, nosy, annoying, or bitter, or they are aggressively ignored. Projectors who use their energy correctly, though, are respected and sought after for their knowledge, talent, and guidance.

Emotional Theme

The best approach for a Projector is to wait to be asked or invited before sharing their advice, opinion, feedback, guidance, or direction. When someone asks, that is an indication that they want the guidance and inherent wisdom of that Projector. (Even if someone is completely unaware that they are asking a Projector, that person is unconsciously reacting to the Projector's energetic configuration.) That person will then hear and appreciate the value of the Projector's input because they were open to receiving it.

The next best approach for the Projector is to wait for some recognition and an opening. Make eye contact and wait for an opportunity to speak without barging into a conversation. Try saying something like the following:

- "I have some experience that may be helpful to you. Would it be all right if I share it with you?"

- "I have some insights about that. May I tell you about them?"

- "Perhaps I could be of help. Would you mind if I try?"

Gentle openings like these facilitate the movement of powerful wisdom out into the world.

Relationships

Projectors in relationships need recognition and attention. It all starts at the very beginning: Projectors need to be invited into a relationship to make the energy flow work. Once a Projector is invited into a relationship, they can simply enjoy being in it. The right initiating energy sets the tone for the relationship.

If you're a Projector in love, you need to be with your partner, but you also need alone time to maintain your energy. You may even find that you feel better when you sleep alone in your own aura. Because, as a Projector, you experience sexual energy from outside of yourself and often in a variable way, you may find that it feels like your partner controls or limits that aspect of your relationship. Conversely, you may also find that sometimes you simply don't have the energy for sex or intimacy. This is usually not personal or a problem in the relationship, just simply a sign that you need some alone time for regeneration and renewal.

If you are the recipient of a Projector's incorrect use of their energy and wisdom, it is easy to feel irritated, turned off, and even repelled. This is normal. Even Projectors can feel turned off by other Projectors! However, you will miss the wisdom and advice that may very well benefit you. Loving and supporting a Projector means giving them the space to feel safe (see Figure 30).

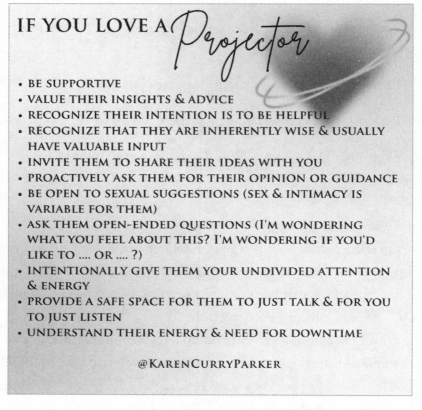

IF YOU LOVE A *Projector*

- BE SUPPORTIVE
- VALUE THEIR INSIGHTS & ADVICE
- RECOGNIZE THEIR INTENTION IS TO BE HELPFUL
- RECOGNIZE THAT THEY ARE INHERENTLY WISE & USUALLY HAVE VALUABLE INPUT
- INVITE THEM TO SHARE THEIR IDEAS WITH YOU
- PROACTIVELY ASK THEM FOR THEIR OPINION OR GUIDANCE
- BE OPEN TO SEXUAL SUGGESTIONS (SEX & INTIMACY IS VARIABLE FOR THEM)
- ASK THEM OPEN-ENDED QUESTIONS (I'M WONDERING WHAT YOU FEEL ABOUT THIS? I'M WONDERING IF YOU'D LIKE TO .... OR .... ?)
- INTENTIONALLY GIVE THEM YOUR UNDIVIDED ATTENTION & ENERGY
- PROVIDE A SAFE SPACE FOR THEM TO JUST TALK & FOR YOU TO JUST LISTEN
- UNDERSTAND THEIR ENERGY & NEED FOR DOWNTIME

@KARENCURRYPARKER

Figure 30: Loving a Projector.

Projectors have a life purpose of managing and guiding others in their process of creation. Projectors are inherently intuitive and wise about others; they can watch Manifestors, Generators, and Manifesting Generators and instantly be conscious of what needs to happen to make their impact more effective and easier. This is a natural part of the Projector's personality. If you watch young children Projectors, they manage their parents and their peers with great awareness as well as clarity. This can often earn them the reputation of being bossy, controlling, or a know-it-all. The reason this inherent wisdom is constantly misunderstood is because collectively we don't know how to make the most of the energy of Projectors.

Projector Children

The greatest gift you can give your Projector is a sense of their own inner wisdom and value. Projector children need to repeatedly show their value, but they need to be taught to wait for recognition. The child also needs to learn to trust that when they wait for the right people who truly value who they are, they can then freely share what they know and have to offer.

Projector children need invitations, and as a parent you may need to facilitate invitations for them. You may even need to help them find jobs and opportunities, because it can be very challenging (and incorrect) for Projectors to go out and find work.

Projectors don't have the same quality of energy as other Types. That means it isn't always easy for them to do physically demanding chores. Find alternative ways for the child to help that suit their Projector nature. Your Projector children will thrive if you give them the opportunity to organize and manage your family.

Your Projector child may find that regular life is taxing and exhausting. You might need to slow down your life and find ways for your Projector to replenish their energy on a weekly basis. For instance, it's not healthy for the Projector child to be deeply committed to lots of after-school activities. Sports and physical activities should be limited, as they may tire more easily than other children.

Work

The Projector Strategy is to wait to be invited into the big opportunities in life. These big invitations come infrequently, perhaps every two to three years. Big opportunities are things like love, marriage, moving, getting a new job, and so on. Projectors don't have to wait for small things, such as going to a movie or going out to eat—but waiting for those big invitations is an important part of helping the Projector find the place in life where they are valued and loved for who they really are.

Projectors are not here to manage and guide everyone. They have their own group of people who waits to be managed by them. To find their people, Projectors must be recognized or invited into sharing their wisdom.

In a society where we are taught to go out and make life happen, waiting for recognition and invitations from others can feel like a painful and agonizingly slow process. Because Projectors are often trained to act differently than their true nature, they can get very busy pushing people to see and recognize them. They often miss the true invitations that come their way because they're too busy doing what they've been trained that they "need" to or "should" be doing by others.

Health

Pushing and forcing will never have a positive outcome for Projectors. In fact, it will always lead to burnout. The more a Projector attempts to struggle their way into being seen or recognized, the more invisible they become.

Not only that, Projectors have a very finite amount of energy and are not meant to work in the traditional way work is designed. If pushed into a situation that doesn't recognize their inherent intuitive gifts or that involves hard physical labor, Projectors will burn out.

Projectors can't make life work for them if they follow the standard definitions of what it takes to be successful in life, although they can be powerful and very successful. (President Obama and President Kennedy are both Projectors.)

When Projectors push or force, they also end up pushing people away rather than attracting them. Because working hard isn't really an option for the limited energy of the Projector, no matter how hard they try, they may often feel that life isn't fair and become bitter.

Projectors must go to bed and relax before they're tired. Discharging all of the energy that was stored through the day takes time—and only then are they able to wind down.

In addition, because very few Projectors are taught how to properly access their energy, of all the groups they can often be the most challenged when it comes to abundance.

Wealth

There are two key factors in creating abundance for the Projector. First, the most important thing that a Projector has to master is their sense of self-worth. A Projector has to wait to be recognized by the right people—the people who value and see them for the gifts they bear. If a Projector is not sitting and waiting for the right people because they question their own value, it makes them bitter and ultimately causes them to waste their wisdom and energy on people who don't value who they are.

Projectors who value themselves enough to wait for the right people to give them invitations are powerfully compelling and frequently turn invitations away. A Projector who values themselves is an abundance magnet.

Second, when a Projector learns to trust the abundant trajectory of the Universe and can wait comfortably for the right invitation to arrive, they conserve their precious energy and feel vibrant, vital, and ready for the invitations when they manifest. Burned-out Projectors, on the other hand, sometimes turn down good invitations if they've wasted their energy pursuing what's not right for them.

When a Projector is living their wealth theme, they are serving as midwives to the world. They guide, coach, and nurture others into fulfilling their roles as initiators and builders. Projectors truly tend to the template of the evolution of the world in every aspect. When Projectors are serving in this capacity, they are strong and powerful blessings to the world around them. They are then magnets for abundant opportunities.

When Projectors first learn their Strategy of waiting for invitations, they often have to dramatically realign their current life. Sometimes, Projectors must keep their day job because they need the money. It can be tricky to keep the traditional flow of income and simultaneously shift to waiting for the right thing to arrive.

It is important for Projectors to do whatever they can in order to stay out of the bitterness—the emotional theme of the Projector. While they're waiting, they need to stay in their joy and follow their bliss. It's not unusual for Projectors to take a deep dive into what brings them joy, only to find that their next invitation is deeply aligned with the joy they've been pursuing!

Projectors are gifted at knowing others, but they're not so good at knowing themselves. Sometimes, Projectors will benefit from having a good friend they can talk to not because they need advice, but because they have to view their decisions in the context of someone else for them to know what is right for them. Talking helps a Projector see themselves and can be crucial to gaining clarity before making a big decision.

Self-care, rest, restoration, and working on self-worth are the most important things Projectors can do to activate their abundance blueprint. When Projectors feel energized and valuable, they transform not only their loved ones and themselves but ultimately the world around them. The truth is that Projectors need more attention and energy from other people than any of the other Types.

Spiritual Theme

Projectors have a deep inner sense of what's possible for the world and know how to direct the necessary energy to bring the intangible into form. They are energy wizards and are, on an unconscious level, constantly realigning and managing the energy flow of the world. This work goes way beyond the tangible physical work of the Generator and Manifestor. This is energy, and the Projector keeps the energy grid of creation in place.

Projectors often report being tired all the time even when they do "nothing." A Projector is never doing nothing. They are in a constant state of holding together the energy grid. Because Projectors know energy so well, they are often involved in energy healing and service-based professions where they are natural healers and helpers.

Many Projectors are magnetic, charismatic recipients of amazing invitations.

Projector Life Purpose Statement: I am here to manage, guide, and direct others towards the fulfillment of their potential. I instinctively know what needs to be done to make the world a better place.

Affirmations

I am a powerful resource for the world. My intuition, insights, awareness, and knowledge help manage and guide the energy of the world and the next phase of growth and evolution on the planet. What I have to offer the world is so powerful, necessary, and valuable that I recognize I am carrying the seeds of evolution within my being. I wait for the right opportunities that reflect the value of what I have to offer. When the opportunity is correct and I am valued, I share my knowledge and wisdom and facilitate the work necessary to build the next phase of the human story. In between opportunities, I rest and replenish my energy so that I'm ready to serve when I am called again.

Projector Examples

The best invitation I have ever received was just recently. My sister, brother, and I have all had tumultuous relationships with our mom.

They aren't currently in communication with her, and I don't really speak with her often. She recently acknowledged the peace she saw within and around me and asked me to share what I've been doing to get to this more serene place. This was not even a month ago, and for the first time (or so it feels), she is actually listening to me, not to respond, but to actually listen. I have now spoken to my mom multiple times since and they are conversations I genuinely enjoy. I've never experienced that in my life with her. She continues to tell me how much I have helped her understand things in a different perspective and that she has a much stronger trust in the Universe. She also said just understanding her emotional authority has helped her tremendously. I've worked on healing a lot of wounds around this relationship and doubt I would be able to have these conversations without doing so.

The combination of that, with being able to utilize the gift of Human Design, both for myself (waiting for the invitation) and providing her with some of the intel that could benefit, has seemed to cause a catalyst. It's as if I'm witnessing a metamorphosis right before my eyes that I never imagined was possible.

—Andrea

The best invitation was the one that led me to a marriage that has (so far) lasted almost thirty-four years. I didn't accept the invitation right away (timing and emotional Definition), but once I was ready, I then asked him. (Gave my Generator husband-to-be something to respond to.)

—Theresa

The following is my favorite Projector story by far:

My ex-husband lived with his mother following our divorce. He stayed with her for a few years to help her with his father who had dementia. Even though he got a lot of pressure to go find a job, he intuitively sensed that he needed to wait for the right invitation.

My ex-husband had a passion for acting and wanted to work in comedy. During the day, he spent a lot of time watching the Turner Network and studying old films.

One day a young, attractive women knocked on the door to his mother's house. She was selling coupon books door-to-door. My ex-husband opened the door and they struck up a conversation. She told my ex-husband that he was super funny and that he should audition for The Comedy Club in downtown Houston.

She worked there in the evenings, and she set up the audition for him. He went to the audition the next day and immediately landed a position doing improv comedy—his dream!

Sometimes, Projectors think that if they do nothing, nothing will happen. This story is a beautiful example of the kind of magic Projectors can experience if they take the time they need in between big invitations to rest and prepare for the next invitation.

The Reflector

Focus: Mirror, community, right place, timing, sensitivity

Strategy: Wait before making decisions, pay attention (wait twenty nine days)

Emotional Theme: Disappointment

Wealth Theme: Living in communities that feel wealthy

Challenges: Trusting that certainty, truth, and solution are more important than anything else

Percentage of People Who Are Reflectors: Less than 1 percent

Role: Reflecting the health and alignment of the people around them

Famous Reflectors: Sandra Bullock, Rosalynn Carter, Uri Geller

Reflectors have all Centers Open and their chart looks almost empty. Reflectors are fully Open to the world and to others. Because there are no Defined Centers by design, Reflectors take in the energy of everybody else, seeing the world

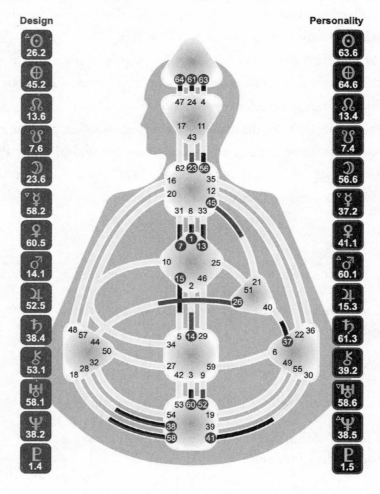

Figure 31: The Reflector.

through others' eyes, sampling a frequency of energy and reflecting it back to them.

Reflectors are like mirrors, and the reflection of other people continually changes their perception. One instant they may feel extremely emotional, while the next moment it's gone. Reflectors may then get all the ideas and a sound sense of knowing where they're going in life, and the next minute it's gone again, and so forth. That's why it's essential for them to carefully choose their friends and partners, because they will have a huge impact on the Reflector's feelings and experience of themselves.

Reflectors have considerably different life experiences than all the other Types, so they may feel lonely and misunderstood. Reflectors can also suffer deep disappointment when having to wait and live through the energy of others.

Due to their emotions, Reflectors require more attention than most all other people and Types. At times, they may feel inadequate and think that they don't fit in anywhere.

The most uncomfortable thing for Reflectors is pressure—especially the pressure to make decisions. For them, it's the most unnatural thing, because Reflectors don't necessarily make decisions. They experience a choice or decision over a cycle of the Moon (twenty-nine days). It's not the same as making a decision with the mind. Reflectors must experience their choice inside themselves over time. Going through the entire cycle gives them the power to be able to realize solutions and right choices.

Common Traps and Challenges

Reflectors, with their Openness and taking in other people's Definition, must wait twenty-nine days before making any major decisions—no matter how certain they may feel about something in the moment.

Reflectors must be in the right geographical location—the place that feels good and like home for their life to feel right. When they are in the right place, they meet the right people, are part of the right community, and life feels aligned. Under these circumstances, making decisions can feel easier and more fulfilling.

Total Openness may make the Reflector almost invisible to others. Not knowing the mechanics of their design, the Reflector may feel deeply disappointed in life. But that very Openness grants the potential for great wisdom and insight for humanity and themself if they learn how to work with it correctly.

Reflectors often struggle with merging in their personal relationships if they don't understand the nature of their Openness and their capacity for deep empathy. Sometimes, the life of a Reflector can get hijacked by the energy of the people surrounding them, and they can lose their direction in life.

Consistency is vital for the Reflector. Reflectors need to have people whose auras they know. It is common for Reflectors to have lifelong friends and to even have trouble disentangling themselves from the energy of their parents simply because Reflectors experience so much inconsistently. The consistency of the people they know makes them feel safe.

Because of the length of time it takes for them to have clarity, Reflectors don't transition quickly and need time to make major life changes, such as leaving home, moving, starting a new job, and getting married.

Strategy

What Reflectors must know and logically understand is that any kind of pressure they experience is detrimental to their health. By taking the time to make important decisions and knowing that the time spent on considering their resolves is how their success is completed, they will realize how vital it is to keep from letting anyone pressure them.

Reflectors are lunar beings, tied to the lunar cycle, so their Strategy—and sometimes their challenge—is to wait twenty-nine days before making any major decisions. During those twenty-nine days, Reflectors should speak with different people about decisions. As a Reflector, you need to have people in your life who will serve as your sounding board, not because you need advice—you don't—but because you need to hear yourself talk about what you are feeling about your choices.

Life for you is an objective experience. As you move through life, repeatedly discovering the truth of "this isn't me," your Openness may be energetically exhausting, so it is important to have your own space where you can relax. The same goes for rest and sleep. The Reflector has an Undefined Sacral; which means ideally they will go to bed as soon as they begin to feel tired and will, if possible, sleep alone.

When Centers are Open, it doesn't mean they are broken or empty. Your mind can easily judge your characteristics as something bad or wrong, but Reflectors carry in their being a deep potential to know the possibilities for humanity. This can be a beautiful thing.

Emotional Theme

Reflectors have the capacity to sense, feel, and know the full potential of the people and the communities around them. Their Openness gives them deep awareness and wisdom about what is possible for the world. It is disappointing for the Reflector to know what's possible and see that the world isn't fulfilling its full potential. Disappointment also comes because the speed of the world and the Reflector's need for ample time to make clear and good decisions don't always align.

When a Reflector fails to take their time in deciding and struggles to find their own energy in the midst of the energy from others, it's easy for them to feel pressured into making a choice quickly. (And, of course, collectively society has little patience for people who need time for clarity.) Consequently, Reflectors can leap into decisions too quickly and then feel disappointed with the long-term consequences of their decisions.

Because of a Reflector's deep capacity to know and connect with the people they love, they prefer to surround themselves with people they've been with for a long time. Many Reflectors also prefer the company of children because the purity of their energy is comforting to Reflectors, who are often disappointed by humanity.

Relationships

Reflectors need people because they are non-energy beings who depend on the energetic connections that others provide them. But they also need alone time so that they may discharge energy that they've absorbed through their nine Open Centers.

There are certain things to remember if you are in a relationship with a Reflector as they discharge others' energy from their system (see Figure 32):

- Love them as they are; don't try to change them, and appreciate their very important role for humanity.

- Reflectors need space, give them the space and time to be themselves.

- Allow them to manage their energy; don't pressure or push them.

- Honor their decision-making sequences.

- Let them speak; Reflectors need to hear their issues and feelings reflected back to them through you.

- Help them recognize when the environment is not healthy for them.

- Understand that they may need you more than you need them.

- Know that you will see the truth about yourself through them; be okay with that revelation.

- Don't take their disappointments personally; it's their nature, their emotion.

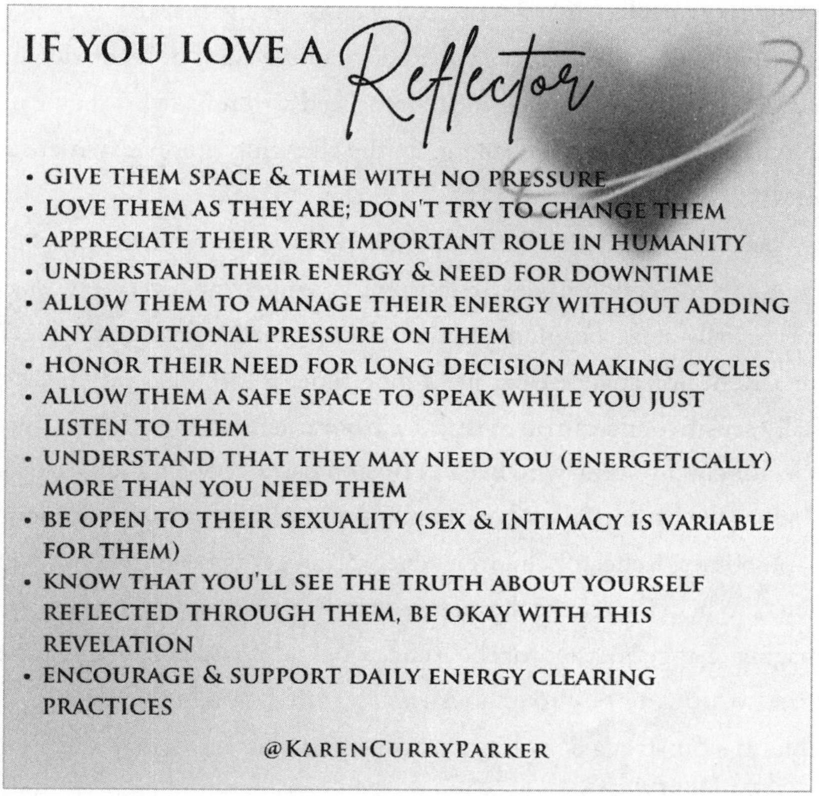

IF YOU LOVE A *Reflector*

- GIVE THEM SPACE & TIME WITH NO PRESSURE
- LOVE THEM AS THEY ARE; DON'T TRY TO CHANGE THEM
- APPRECIATE THEIR VERY IMPORTANT ROLE IN HUMANITY
- UNDERSTAND THEIR ENERGY & NEED FOR DOWNTIME
- ALLOW THEM TO MANAGE THEIR ENERGY WITHOUT ADDING ANY ADDITIONAL PRESSURE ON THEM
- HONOR THEIR NEED FOR LONG DECISION MAKING CYCLES
- ALLOW THEM A SAFE SPACE TO SPEAK WHILE YOU JUST LISTEN TO THEM
- UNDERSTAND THAT THEY MAY NEED YOU (ENERGETICALLY) MORE THAN YOU NEED THEM
- BE OPEN TO THEIR SEXUALITY (SEX & INTIMACY IS VARIABLE FOR THEM)
- KNOW THAT YOU'LL SEE THE TRUTH ABOUT YOURSELF REFLECTED THROUGH THEM, BE OKAY WITH THIS REVELATION
- ENCOURAGE & SUPPORT DAILY ENERGY CLEARING PRACTICES

@KARENCURRYPARKER

Figure 32: Loving a Reflector.

Reflectors can easily merge with the people around them. In relationships, they can easily match their partners. It is easy for Reflectors to not realize that they are giving up their own needs and wants because they have lost their energetic connection to themselves and their own needs.

Reflector Children

Reflector children present a unique set of challenges for parents. Raising a Reflector child requires patience, love, and an awareness that your child may need more attention and energy than your other children.

The first thing Reflector children need is consistency. Because so much of the Reflector experience is variable, the consistency of the auras of their friends, loved ones, and caregivers is vital. These children need to know who they can trust, and who will be steady and unchanging in the changing energy experience of the Reflector.

This need for consistency can make the Reflector child appear to be clingy or needy. Reflector children need consistent caregivers and very few major life changes, especially at the beginning of their lives. Cataclysmic changes like divorce can leave a Reflector child reeling for a long time. Reflector children are deeply emotionally sensitive and can often react to major events that happen on the planet. One Reflector child I know who lived in Boston had a very emotional breakdown the day before the Boston Marathon bombing and was inconsolable for more than a week. Sometimes, Reflector children benefit from getting energy work by skilled practitioners to help the release the energy that they hold in their bodies.

Managing change is easier for the Reflector child if you are patient and understanding. Also, do your best to establish a new foundation in their lives as quickly as possible. If you struggle with consistency and routine, it may deeply impact your Reflector child. Setting routines and sticking to them help the Reflector child feel safe and stable.

Reflector children need to feel good in their space. Once they are seven or older when the aura is mature, Reflector children fare better sleeping in their own room, away from others. This gives their energy field time to decompress and release the energy of others.

Because Reflectors have an Open Sacral Center, some Reflector children will struggle with hard physical chores. The best way to help a Reflector get things done is to do it with them. This can sometimes even be true for homework and other activities.

Finally, Reflector children talk a lot and need to talk to know what they're thinking and feeling. As a parent of a Reflector, you need to allow your child the freedom to dump out their thoughts and resist the urge to give them advice or guidance unless they ask you. They're not asking for guidance; they are simply talking to get clarity. If you give them guidance without being asked, it will trigger their own tendency toward feeling inadequate, or they will feel controlled.

Work

Like the Projector and Manifestor Types, Reflectors do not have sustainable energy. Only Generators and Manifesting Generators have that Type of energy. So, with Reflectors, they are not wired to work a typical job sustainably, which may be an issue in relationships and in earning a living.

While Reflectors can amplify a lot of power and seemingly have a lot of intense energy, they cannot sustain that energy over time. They need cycles of rest and renewal like all Open Sacral Types.

Their need to talk and their need to take time to make good choices can sometimes cause them pain in the workplace. Once they are recognized for their empathy and the awareness they bring to the workplace, they can assume their right role of reflecting the health of the business and serve as the powerful barometers that they are.

Reflectors in the workplace can be visionaries and can express the potential of the business as they carry the awareness of what's possible in their energy field.

Health

There are three main factors to staying healthy if you are a Reflector.

First, you need to be in an environment that feels good to you, and the people in your environment need to be healthy. Because you are so sensitive to others and the experiences of others, if you are in an environment where people aren't making healthy choices, that will deeply impact you.

Second, you need good sleep and rest. Like all non-Sacral Types, Reflectors sleep best alone and need to be in the energy of their own aura at night to stay vital.

Reflectors need to be in bed before they are tired and rest in a prone position until they fall asleep.

Third, you need to take your time to make the decisions that are right for you. If you feel pressured to decide before you're ready, it may end up being the wrong choice and the pressure and struggle to try to feel "right" about the decision can deeply impact your physical and emotional health.

Wealth

Much like with health, so much of the Reflector experience with wealth depends on their environment. Their ability to create wealth and be in the flow of abundance will be influenced deeply by the people they associate with and where they live their life. Ideally, the environment offers a wealth of abundant energy.

A Reflector can make more money and create a strong financial foundation when they take their time to make good choices. Fast-paced moneymaking plans don't always play out well for the Reflector because they need time to make good choices. Slow down and only invest in opportunities that afford you the time to be clear on things.

Because Reflectors are non-Sacral beings, they need to consciously save and create a financial cushion for themselves to support them when they need a cycle of rest. Starting young with a powerful saving strategy benefits the Reflector the most.

Spiritual Theme

Reflectors are here to be our karmic mirrors. Their life experience and their reflection to us reveal where we are in our evolutionary process. The Reflectors in our lives show us how close we are to fulfilling our potential and let us know the emotional maturity and alignment we are experiencing by living it and demonstrating it in their own reflected experience.

The heart of the Reflector carries within it the potential for our optimal evolution and the story of what else is possible for humanity.

Reflector Life Purpose Statement: I am here to serve as a barometer for the world. With my feelings, experiences, and actions, I embody the energy of those around me and reflect back to them how aligned they are with the fulfillment of their potential.

Affirmations

I am a karmic mirror. Through my experience and my expression of the energy around me I reflect back to others their potential and their misalignment. Through my reflection, others can see what they need to bring back into alignment to fulfill their path. I understand the depth of the potential of possibility for humanity. I know that it is not my job to fix the world but to simply mirror back the current energies. I trust in divine timing and know that with time the potential of the world will be fulfilled. I am patient and honoring of myself. I give myself the time I need to make right choices and to place myself in the right location with the right people. I trust my inner sense of feeling at home in the place where I belong, and I stay aligned with where I feel most at home.

Reflector Examples

It's hard for me to live like a Reflector but it's so worth it, even though sometimes I have to lie. When I first got accepted into graduate school, I was under a lot of pressure to say yes quickly. I knew that I needed time to get clear, so I told them yes even though I wasn't sure. I gave myself permission to back out of my decision if I needed to, even though I felt guilty for lying. After a couple months, going to graduate school felt right and I was able to relax and prepare.

Learning to wait has saved me a lot of heartache, even though sometimes people get frustrated with me for not being very fast or seemingly decisive.

—Sarah Parker

Working with Your Personality Type

Now that you've been introduced to the details about each Type and you've identified via your chart which Type you are, you can begin to personally explore this in more depth. This section will take you through a series of reflections and journaling prompts, which will culminate in your writing the first part of your personal statement that will allow you to integrate the lessons of your chart in story form.

Your Type Contemplations

1. What is your Type?

_____

_____

2. What is the Strategy for your Type? How do you see yourself already reflecting this Strategy in your life? What are some ways you could implement this Strategy more often?

_____

_____

3. What are some common challenges for your Type? Have you experienced any of these yourself? What can you do to overcome these challenges?

_____

_____

4. What do you need in your interpersonal and work relationships? What changes in your current relationships would help you to get your needs met? How do you feel your Type may affect how you relate?

_____

_____

5. What is your creative style? Does your current life reflect the creative style of your Type? What changes might you make to support your Type's creative style?

_____

_____

6. What is the spiritual theme for your Type? How can you deepen your alignment with your spiritual purpose?

_____

_____

Your Story

Your story is the first part of your personal statement. Fill in the following blanks with the information you've learned from your Human Design chart and this chapter. When we reach the end of this book, you'll put several of these statements together to form your personal Life Purpose Statement (see page 257).

Once you have the following information filled in, I recommend taking some time to sit with it before moving on to the next chapter. See if any emotions, memories, or thoughts surface. You may also wish to meditate on this, if that's a part of your practice, to integrate this knowledge into your being.

I, _____ (name), a _____ (Your Human Design Type), am here to serve the world by _____ _____ (the Life Purpose of your Human Design Type).

Chapter 3

PROFILES

While your Type gives you an overview of your key strengths and Strategy for pursuing your dreams and participating in life in the very best way possible, your Profile tells you about major life themes that you will encounter as you navigate the world. In this way, Profiles illustrate a slightly different way in which your personality interacts with the river of life. Put another way, your Type can be thought of as being your character, and your Profile is your role in this lifetime. Knowing your Profile can help you move toward fulfilling your life purpose.

Your Profile helps you understand your learning style, what you need to feel secure in your decision-making, how you relate to yourself and others, and how you share your gifts with the world.

There are twelve different personality Profiles in the Human Design system.

Your Profile looks like a fraction on your Human Design chart (see Figure 33). Each number represents specific archetypical themes that influence your experience of the world. These numbers inform you about what's necessary in order to feel confident and strong in making good decisions and creating a life you love.

The first number represents how you share your gifts with the world. The second number represents what you need to feel secure and grounded before you can share your gifts. These two numbers operate in conjunction with each other.

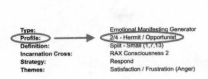

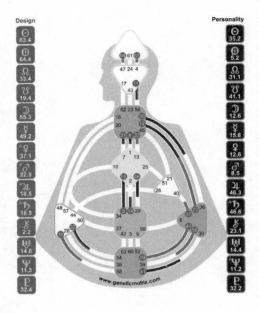

Figure 33: The Profile on the Human Design chart.

The needs of both archetype themes in your Profile must be met for you to feel at peace with your life and your choices.

Human Design shows us that growth often involves mastering challenges and finding ways to harmonize between the different parts of yourself. Many of the archetype themes within the two lines of a Profile present a conundrum—two different energy themes that seem to be at odds with each other. It is in finding ways to work with both of these themes in your life that you can deepen your self-mastery, resilience, and self-acceptance.

When you live the highest expression of the two lines in your Profile, then you will see that both archetypes can complement each other and support you in fulfilling your life purpose.

The Six Profile Lines

Six Profile lines of Investigator, Hermit, Experiential Learner, Opportunist, Teacher, and Role Model are present in each of the twelve Profiles (see Figure 34).

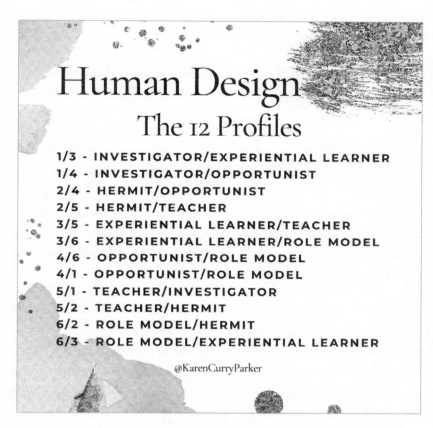

Human Design
The 12 Profiles

1/3 - INVESTIGATOR/EXPERIENTIAL LEARNER
1/4 - INVESTIGATOR/OPPORTUNIST
2/4 - HERMIT/OPPORTUNIST
2/5 - HERMIT/TEACHER
3/5 - EXPERIENTIAL LEARNER/TEACHER
3/6 - EXPERIENTIAL LEARNER/ROLE MODEL
4/6 - OPPORTUNIST/ROLE MODEL
4/1 - OPPORTUNIST/ROLE MODEL
5/1 - TEACHER/INVESTIGATOR
5/2 - TEACHER/HERMIT
6/2 - ROLE MODEL/HERMIT
6/3 - ROLE MODEL/EXPERIENTIAL LEARNER

@KarenCurryParker

Figure 34: The Twelve Profiles with the Six Profile Lines.

Let's review the basic definitions for each of these:

Line 1: The Investigator needs information and feels safe when they have sufficient data.

Line 2: The Hermit needs alone time to process experiences and to reset their energy. Line 2 Profiles need space to feel good and grounded. Once hermits have taken time away, other people energetically perceive they're ready to be invited out to be a part of the community again.

Line 3: The Experiential Learner must experiment with their ideas and be allowed to make mistakes without judgment.

Line 4: The Opportunist builds a foundation of friendships and needs to network as well as share. They need to know what's next and be prepared to feel safe.

Line 5: The Teacher teaches whatever they've experienced in life. They are karmic mirrors and often see the best and the potential in others. It's through relationships with Line 5 Profiles that others discover what they need to heal the most within themselves and how they can fulfill their potential. They must trust that you will see the truth about them to feel safe, and sometimes will hide their truth very deeply when you first get to know them.

Line 6: The Role Model literally models for others what they are here to share with the world and need to feel that what they are participating in is worth their effort to find meaning and energy in life. They travel through three distinct life phases: a youthful phase of experimentation and experiential learning; a long cycle of healing, growth, and studying; and a cycle of living what they've learned.

Now, let's take a more in-depth look at each of these archetypes.

Line 1: The Investigator

The following are the characteristics present in Line 1 Profiles:

Purpose: To be a resource of knowledge, data, and information for others

Needs: Having enough information to make a good decision

Drive: Curiosity

Fear: Not knowing enough or fear of the unknown

Challenge: To not let fear of the unknown prevent personal growth or evolution; to learn to trust that knowledge will come when the time is right

Mastery: To follow curiosity and investigate information, building a foundation of knowledge that can be shared with others

When Unbalanced: You might fail to move forward with choices and decisions, wrapped up in investigating information. You might let fear of the unknown paralyze forward momentum.

Line 1 energy is all about knowing enough to feel like you have enough information to move forward with confidence. If you have a Line 1 in your Profile, you are curious. The internet was made for you, and your favorite thing to do is to investigate.

The Investigator questions everything. They want to know who, how, and why. Before making a decision, they must know as much as possible. If you go on a trip, for example, you like to have a plan and maybe own several guidebooks for the region to which you're traveling (which you've read several times).

Knowledge is security for Line 1 Profiles. The more you know, the more you feel like you're able to adapt to whatever is in front of you. If you are facing any big changes in your life, such as moving to a new place or buying a house, you need to feel like you've investigated every aspect of the decision to feel confident that you know what to expect.

Ultimately, the purpose of your curious nature is to understand enough to be able to share what you learned with others. You are a resource to your friends and family because you've investigated all the options.

Line 1 Profiles fear not knowing enough, and they fear the unknown. If you're a Line 1, your need for information can sometimes make it difficult for you to be spontaneous or to make a quick decision in the moment. If you feel like you don't have enough information, it can cause you to feel deeply uncomfortable.

You're unlikely to trust your gut if you don't have information first. It's important for you to understand that needing information is not a flaw; it's how the Investigator moves through the world and makes good choices. Being spontaneous is not necessarily healthy if you don't have a foundation of information first.

Contemplation

- How do you manage fear of the unknown?

- Are you letting your fears keep you from moving forward?

Affirmation

I am a resource of information for others. My depth of knowledge and research gives me the confidence that I am able to engineer solutions to the challenges in front of me. I give myself ample time to explore my curiosity and to gather the depth of information that I need to make an informed choice. I trust that the depth of my understanding will help me know what I need to know when I need to know it, and I relax and trust my internal database.

Line 2: The Hermit

The following characteristics are present in Line 2 Profiles:

Purpose: To integrate knowledge, energy, and wisdom, then wait to be summoned by others to share this wisdom

Needs: Alone time to rest, process experiences, and regenerate, to be ready when it's time to share

Drive: To master the balance between alone time and being out in the world

Fear: Disappearing and being isolated

Challenge: Balance the need for self-renewal with the need to serve the world

Mastery: Integrating the need for alone time and integration and knowing when to respond to the needs of others; finding a balance between retreating and responding to the world

When Unbalanced: Retreating too deeply from life or burning out

Line 2's energy is about needing ample alone time to process and prepare for whatever is next in life. Doing without it can lead to feeling overwhelmed and overstimulated.

The energy present in Line 2 Profiles means they are very sensitive. As a Line 2 Profile, you're designed to respond to the needs of others. Your energy keeps you aware of the energy of others so that you're ready to give them what they need when they ask. This constant state of being dialed in to the needs of others requires that you get the necessary alone time to rest your energy and be ready for what's next.

The challenge is to not retreat too much. You might deeply long for and fantasize about going to a hermitage far away from others. But there's an irony in that, because as soon as you feel rested enough, it's almost as though your aura signals to the world that you're ready for whatever is next. Others sense this and will call you out into the world to serve again. This call or sense of obligation to give to others can sometimes cause you to fail to take the alone time you need, leading you to burnout and resentment. The trick to mastering your Line 2 Profile is to find the right balance between self-care, restoration, and going out into the world and creating impact. You must learn how to do all of it.

Contemplation

- What is your Strategy for self-renewal? What do you need to take time for yourself?

- Are you hiding out? Are you avoiding living true to your purpose? Are there any bold steps that you need to take to share yourself with the world?

Affirmation

I am uniquely designed to respond to the needs of others. I sense and feel what they need, and I give and share freely. In order for me to serve the world at my highest level, I need alone time to recharge and integrate. I nurture myself as an essential aspect of amplifying my ability to give to others. I trust that when I retreat and take care of myself, I will be called out by others when it's time for me to serve again. When I am called out, I will have the resources I need to share with the world, because I've replenished my own essence first.

Line 3: The Experiential Learner

The following characteristics are present in Line 3 Profiles:

Purpose: To explore and experience possibilities and share these experiences with others to protect and serve them

Needs: To experiment and try things

Drive: To try things to see what works and what doesn't; to discover how to make things better based on experience

Fear: Failure

Challenge: Allowing for experimentation and exploration for the sake of discovering what works (and what doesn't); conquering any fear of failing

Mastery: To fearlessly experiment and explore for the sake of discovering what works best; to realize that mistakes are simply part of the learning process and that perfection is found through experimentation

When Unbalanced: Failing to try something new out of fear of failure; self-judging for making too many mistakes

The mantra of Line 3 Profiles is to *try everything*. As a Line 3 Profile, it's your energy's nature to need to experience something before you can truly understand it.

Line 3 Profiles are experiential learners. Your gift is knowing what works and what doesn't based on your experience. Your energy is a powerful resource for the world, as you share what you know based on your own trials and explorations.

Your challenge is to not judge your experiences and explorations as failures. In a world that expects perfection, it's easy for you to feel like you are always screwing up. As a child, you may have left behind a trail of experiences that simply didn't measure up to other people's expectations of success. A fear of falling short of such expectations can often cause you to refrain from trying new things and to shut down your need for exploration. If you let this fear of failure stop you, however, you are shutting down a vital part of your personality.

You're here to experiment, explore, and push the boundaries of what's possible. You're not always going to get it right the first time. But with repeated explorations and experimentations, you can become an expert, understanding how to troubleshoot an experience and find the best ways to make things work.

Your experience provides you with wisdom and knowledge to share. Your explorations give others the information they need to make effective and informed choices. In addition, they won't have to work out the bugs because you've already done it for them!

Contemplation

- Do you allow yourself to try new things? How do you feel when things don't go right the first time? Do you judge yourself, or do you let yourself continue to work toward finding the solution?

- How have people reacted to your creative process in the past? Do past judgments from others cause you to be shy about trying something new now?

- What would your life be like if you allowed yourself to follow your relentless curiosity and need to explore?

Affirmation

I am an explorer. My curiosity inspires me to try all kinds of things. My experiences teach me what works and what doesn't. I am an expert who knows many things based on my experimentation and exploration. I have never made a mistake in my life. All my failed experiments are simply opportunities for me to discover how to make a process more effective and efficient. I am a wealth of knowledge for others. I use my experiences to help others know what to do.

Line 4: The Opportunist

The following characteristics are present in Line 4 Profiles:

Purpose: To build and be a part of a community to prepare the way for sharing and spreading of ideas

Needs: Stability and consistency

Drive: To build the support and opportunities necessary to be prepared for any situation that may arise; to always have a backup plan ready just in case

Fear: The fear of loss and limbo

Challenge: To learn to navigate the unexpected with trust, grace, and ease; to know that knowledge will present itself when the time is right

Mastery: Knowing how to make a change; being ready for the future; using connections and friendships to build a network of opportunities personally and for others; and being a spirit of information

When Unbalanced: Letting the fear of not knowing and loss become overwhelming; being afraid of making or facing change

The energy of Line 4 Profiles requires the stability of knowing what's next to navigate changes in life. Sometimes, the Line 4 Profile is referred to as the Opportunist, but you are not opportunistic in the negative way most tend to think of. Rather, you need to know the details of what's lined up next for the process of change and transformation to feel easy to you.

If you are a Line 4 Profile, it means that you don't like to quit a job until you have another job lined up. You don't want to move or sell your house until you know where you're going to live next. Being in a state of limbo can feel very unsettling for you. Because of this, Line 4 Profiles tend to be experts at constantly creating contingency plans, so they are ready for any unexpected life change.

The gift of being a Line 4 Profile is stability. You are trustworthy, your relationships run deep, and you make changes deliberately and with lots of planning and troubleshooting before you pull the trigger to act. People rely on you, and you are often the one they turn to for support and encouragement. You are also often a spirit of information for your friends and family because you're always prepared for the next potential opportunity—or disaster.

Knowing what and which people to trust is essential for your Line 4 energy. You feel safe and confident when you are surrounded by people you know and have confidence in. Your friendships tend to last a long time.

Sudden, unexpected change can't always be avoided and is part of life. The challenge for a Line 4 Profile is to learn how to navigate change with grace even if you don't know what's next. Part of your life lesson is to learn to flow with change without always having the answers you crave, and to not fear the process of change and transformation.

Your ability to be prepared for any situation, change, and circumstance makes you highly adaptable and capable of navigating change with ease and grace.

Contemplation

- How do you navigate change? Do you trust the process? Do you make changes with grace? What is your process for making changes in your life?

- What kinds of stability do you need to feel confident in your life? Do you have the foundation that you need? Do you need to strengthen this foundation?

- Which people do you trust? What do you trust? What do you need to do to deepen your relationships and trust?

Affirmation

I need a strong and stable foundation for my life. I take my time and prepare for what's ahead. My knowledge, resilience, and trust that I generate help others rely on and trust me. Trust is essential for me to feel safe and grounded in my relationships. I am experienced at the process of change, and my experience of knowing how to bring about change makes me adaptable, even if I don't know what's next. I prepare for change by creating plans for all possibilities. I need plans to feel confident in my ability to facilitate an easy transition. I trust that I'll know what I'll need to know when I need to know it, and I know how to find the information and create the opportunities I need to make changes with grace.

Line 5: The Teacher

The following characteristics are present in Line 5 Profiles:

Purpose: To teach, lead, and inspire

Needs: To be genuinely seen, heard, and valued by others

Drive: To experience and learn from life; to share knowledge with others

Fear: Not being or feeling truly seen or heard

Challenge: To learn to read people carefully; to engage in relationships that reflect one's truth and value; to not let fear of the projection of others impede an inspiring leader and teacher

Mastery: The ability to reflect back to others their potential; to lead, teach, and inspire others to fulfill their potential

When Unbalanced: Taking the projections and expectations of others personally; letting the pain of the projection field thwart one's natural role as a leader

The energy of Line 5 Profiles is incredibly powerful. When you have this energy, your aura is compelling; people are drawn to you. You might find that it's common for people to come up to you and ask you if they know you from somewhere. This isn't necessarily a pickup line as much as it is that your energy field is attractive and people are drawn to it.

You're probably not actually doing anything to draw people to you. In fact, most Line 5 Profiles don't want attention. But your energy field has a big purpose, and attracting people to you is part of that purpose. You are a leader, and your energy field communicates to others that you have answers and information that they need — even if they don't know exactly what it is that they need from you.

Your energy presents certain challenges that can sometimes be hard to interpret until you really understand the nature of your purpose as a Line 5 Profile. Your energy field is somewhat of a mirror. People will see in you, or through their interaction with you, what they need to heal within themselves. This is known as the *projection field* in Human Design.

The projection field sets you up in life to sometimes find yourself in relationships where people have fantasies or expectations about who they think you are, what they think you promised, and what they think you're up to. You've probably been surprised and even saddened by this your whole life, as it may have left you feeling like no one really sees you or gets you. The purpose of these projections is for people to have an opportunity to see for themselves what they need to heal and take responsibility for within themselves.

Your projection field may often leave you hiding out in their lives. The pain of having been projected upon, because you weren't with the right people, can cause many Line 5 Profiles to play their cards close to their chests. This isolation, or shutting down, can often amplify the pain of feeling not seen or heard.

It is essential for you, as a Line 5 Profile, to ensure that you are discerning about your relationships. When you are with the right people, you have an innate ability to see the gifts of others and help them fulfill their potential. Your ability to see the possibilities for people makes you a healer and a leader. Your energy draws them into the vision of possibility that you hold, and your wisdom helps them do the work necessary to expand their potential. You need to be with those who are willing to see your projection field as a mirror and who will not blame you or have false expectations about what you can do for them. If you find yourself in a community of people with false expectations, you must value yourself enough to set good boundaries and change the nature of your relationships.

Contemplation

- How comfortable do you feel being seen and heard? Are you hiding out?

- Are you in relationships and in a community that values you and your wisdom?

- What are you here to inspire and lead people to do? What do you need to do to strengthen your connection to your bigger vision?

Affirmation

I am a teacher, leader, and healer. Through my interactions with others, I reveal people's potentials, mirror back to them what they need to do to heal and align themselves, and what they need to do to fulfill their destiny. I hold space for this reflection without taking responsibility for it. I am deliberate, clear, and intentional with my communication because I know my words are influential and powerful. I am discerning with the company I keep. I surround myself with people who know their value and respect my value.

Line 6: The Role Model

The following characteristics are present in Line 6 Profiles. Note that Line 6 Profiles have a unique life trajectory that consists of three very different life phases.

Purpose: To experience, watch, and learn how to live authentically; to quietly model authenticity for others

Needs: To live in alignment with one's life purpose

Drive: To make the world a better place

Fear: The fear of failing one's life purpose

Challenges:

Phase One: Allow experimentation and exploration for the sake of discovering what works (and what doesn't); overcome the fear of failing

Phase Two: Make time to rest, heal, learn, contemplate, and process life experiences

Phase Three: Let the intelligence of life reveal the right next step to take to fulfill one's life purpose; remember that how a life is lived is more important than what is accomplished

Mastery:

Phase One: To fearlessly experiment and explore for the sake of discovering what works best; to realize that mistakes are simply part of the experiential learning process and that perfection is found through experimentation

Phase Two: To integrate all knowledge and insights; to realize that this cycle is essential for well-being and to allow time for rest, healing, learning, and exploring the internal creative plane; to master being at peace with trusting the unfolding of life and life plans and to surrender to that unfolding

Phase Three: To live as a master of aligned and authentic living; to trust that modeling for others what living in alignment and being relentlessly authentic looks like have profound effects; to show the world how to live by walking the talk

When Unbalanced:

Phase One: Avoiding trying something new due to fear of failure; judging mistakes

Phase Two: Failing to rest, heal, or process because of the pressure of needing to do what's next in life; pushing too hard and hustling too much, and ultimately burning out

Phase Three: Using will, force, and mental machinations to compel a position of leadership; believing that the ends justify the means, and failing to live in integrity; caving to the fear of failure

Each of these phases is an essential part of your maturing process as a Line 5 Profile and necessary for you to fulfill your life purpose of being a model for authentic living.

The first phase of life lasts from birth until about age thirty—your first Saturn return. In this phase, you are designed to experience and explore life much like a Line Three Profile. Mistakes are not present in this phase, only experiences that will help you learn about what works and what doesn't.

The second phase occurs between the ages of thirty to fifty. During this phase, you have several tasks you must complete in order to be ready to fully step into your role model identity. This second cycle is called "being on the roof" in Human Design.

When you are on the roof, you are healing from your adventures in the first phase of your life. You are watching and learning about what others do to create success, and you're storing up energy and resting so that you'll be ready to launch into the third and final phase of your life.

This being on the roof phase is a great time for you to focus and draw inward. You may find that during this phase your energy is quite different than the energy from your youth. It might not feel like you have as much energy as you had back in your twenties. You may prefer a quiet night at home with close friends as compared to going out into the world and trying something new. Small talk can feel hard in this phase.

Many Line 6 Profiles worry that they are depressed or that they've lost their edge during this phase. You may feel driven to do something big and bold, but at the same time you may feel that you don't have the energy or that nothing seems to work out the way you imagined. If you don't learn to relax and allow yourself to simply be with this part of your maturing cycle, it's very easy to burn out by pushing too hard. Rest assured, things do get better.

Your third and final life phase happens around age fifty, when you come off the roof and emerge as a role model for others. At this stage of your life, you have experienced what has worked and what hasn't, you've learned and healed, and now you're ready to show others how to be in alignment with their authentic selves by walking the talk and living true to your authentic self.

As a Line 6 Profile, you have a couple challenges. It's common to feel like you're not getting things done fast enough, that your (mis)adventures are costing you precious time, and that you are failing your life purpose.

During the roof phase, you are challenged by the feeling of not wanting to connect with the world and not having the energy to do what you feel you must do to fulfill your purpose. As difficult as it can seem, the most essential thing you must do is learn, study, and find ways to be patient. The goal of this phase is for you to heal and process your past experiences and to be energetically strong for the later phases of your life. Many Line 6 Profiles feel a lot of anxiety and pressure, especially around ages forty-five to fifty. To stay healthy, Line 6 Profiles who are on the roof have to accept that their time is coming, but they need to arrive at their destiny refreshed, healed, and wise. If they push against the timing, they run the risk of becoming depleted and unable to do what they need to do when it is actually their time for impact.

The third and final stage is much less challenging than the first two, but if you are a mature Line 6 Profile and you still feel like you haven't found your purpose, the same frustration that has followed you your whole life will feel even more amplified and potentially despairing at this stage.

If you are a Line 6 Profile, you have a lot less wiggle room in your destiny, meaning, you have more of a fixed fate than some of the other Profiles. This gives you a deep sense of purpose that helps you dig deep and devote yourself to fulfilling your life's mission. Your energy gives you a drive that many others long for.

It is essential that you also remember that play and having fun are an essential part of cultivating creativity and joy. Living your purpose is important, but finding that balance between saving the world and enjoying your life is essential in helping you stay vital and energized.

Contemplation

- How do you feel about experimenting and getting it wrong? How do you feel about resting? Do you trust that when the time is right, you'll get to fulfill your life purpose?

- What does integrity mean to you? What does walking your talk mean to you? Are you living authentically? What needs to change to bring your life into alignment?

- What phase of life are you in? Are you in alignment with your current phase? Are you resisting? What needs to change for you to be in alignment?

- How do you manage your fear of failing at your life's mission? Do you see evidence of where you are getting it right?

Affirmation

I am a role model of authentic living. Me being the full, unlimited expression of who I am is my life purpose. Others look to me to see what authentic living and integrity look like. My life has given me experience and the wisdom to show others how to live in alignment with the right timing, authentic self-expression, honesty, self-generosity, and in service to the world. There is nothing that I have to do unless I am called to do something. It is simply in me being myself that I show the world how to live.

Conclusion

Each line in each Profile is designed to support the others. You need to fulfill the needs of both of your lines to fulfill the purpose of those lines in your Profile. Your overall goal is to always fulfill your life purpose.

In theory, the first number in your Profile provides the foundation for the expression of the second number. So, for example, the 1/3 Profile (the Investigator/Experiential Learner) needs a strong foundation of information before they can embark on the journey of experiencing and exploring their ideas.

In reality, it's often hard to tease out which of the two needs is foundational and which is expressive. In addition, some of the line themes in your Profile can at times feel as if they are at odds with each other. The truth is that all charts have a certain amount of internal struggle associated with them. These struggles are designed as growth catalysts in your life journey. Sometimes, you must push against parts of yourself—you must struggle to find the balance between all the facets of the diamond that is you and discover ways to harmonize all the parts of yourself. Doing so is the spirit of maturity and true wisdom in your chart.

The bottom line? Make sure you take the time to meet both needs of the lines in your Profile. Accomplishing this will help you make good, solid decisions and feel confident and aligned, which will help you fulfill your life purpose.

Your Story

Fill in the following blanks with the information you've learned from your Human Design chart.

I need, learn, share, and grow in my ability to give to the world through _____ _____ (conscious line of your Profile). I need _____ (unconscious line of your Profile) to be able to do so.

Chapter 4

YOUR ENERGY CENTERS

The unique configuration of your Centers is analogous to a plan for the electrical wiring of your house. When your home was built or remodeled, the electricians followed a blueprint to lay the wiring that runs energy into the rooms. The plan shows how much energy flows to each specific location and where to place sockets and outlets.

What is not drawn on this plan is what you're going to actually plug in to the sockets and how you're going to use the electricity in the kitchen. The electrician doesn't necessarily know whether you're going to plug a blender or toaster oven into the socket.

Your Human Design chart is like the electrical blueprint. The Centers are like the plugs and outlets. You can see from your blueprint how the energy flows, but it's up to you to explore what you're going to plug in and how you utilize the chart.

Defined Centers

As mentioned in Chapter 1, your Energy Centers can be Defined or Undefined. When they are colored on your Human Design chart, they are Defined, meaning you carry and experience these energies all the time. Your Defined Centers represent parts of your personal story that you will explore, learn about, and eventually share with the world as part of your life's curriculum. Your Defined Centers are part of what you're here to share with the world.

Which of your Centers are Defined? List them here, then color them in on Figure 35.

_____

Undefined Centers

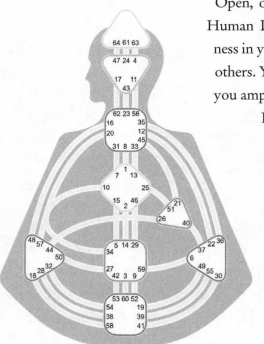

Open, or Undefined, Centers are white on your Human Design chart. Wherever you have Openness in your chart is where you absorb energy from others. You don't just absorb this energy, however; you amplify it.

Because you experience Openness from outside yourself, these energies are always inconsistent—and you may mistakenly think they belong to you instead of to others. The more Openness you have in your chart, the more sensitive you are, and the greater the reality that you will become wise about the potential of the human experience.

Figure 35: A Blank Human Design Chart.

Open Centers create predictable behavioral themes. These themes sometimes cause you to engage in self-defeating patterns and habits that hold you back from accessing the wisdom that your Openness brings you. These themes may also cause you to act out in ways that are not in alignment with your true self.

Which of your Centers are Undefined? List them here.

Now let's discuss the Centers themselves.

Head Center Energy

The Head Center is the Center for ideas and inspiration. This is the Center that regulates those seeds of ideas, sparks of curiosity, and epiphanies that spur us to try to figure out how to turn ideas into reality.

The higher purpose of the Head Center is to use inspiration to generate ideas. Our contemplations and inspirations are not designed to be acted upon, but to be used to keep us in an inspired state, preparing us to explore our outer reality with curiosity and presence.

This Center is associated with the crown chakra, representing the connection between our human self and our higher self.

Defined Head Center

If your Head Center is Defined (see Figure 36), it will be yellow on your chart. If it is Defined, part of your life's purpose is to inspire others. This isn't something you actively do, however; you simply carry an energy that encourages others.

Challenge

There really isn't a challenge associated with the Defined Head Center. Do be mindful, though, of your mental energy because of the effect is has on others.

Contemplation

- What practices could you cultivate to support an uplifting and inspiring mindset?

- Have you noticed times when your presence is inspiring to others?

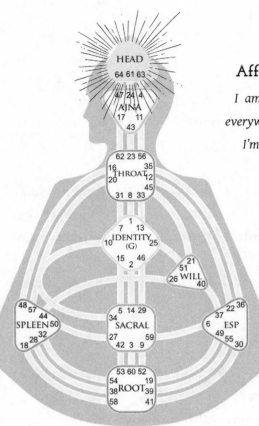

Figure 36: The Defined
Head Center.

Affirmation

I am inspired and inspiring. I spread inspiration everywhere I go, and I share my ideas with others when I'm asked to do so.

I am here to be wise about *inspiring others and sharing ideas.*

Undefined Head Center

If your Head Center is white on your chart, it's Undefined or Open (see Figure 37). The Head Center is one of two Centers that can create pressure in your life if they are Open. (The Root Center is the other.) Most people have an Open Head Center. Having an Open Head Center can place you under mental pressure to try to figure out how to turn the inspirations you are amplifying into reality.

The real purpose of the Head Center is not to figure things out, but rather to be inspired and to use that inspiration to stir up excitement and anticipation. The excitement that your dreams stir up programs you to start seeking ways to fulfill those dreams in the world around you.

All Human Design Types must wait before creating what they want in life. The dreams of your Open Head Center inspire you to start looking in your outer world for the next step to making your ideas a reality.

Challenge

The challenge of having an Undefined or Open Head Center is to manage your inspiration carefully. Just because you have an idea doesn't mean you must make it something you work to create. The Open Head Center needs to dream and be inspired. Being inspired is an energy that requires tending. Your job, when you have an Open Head Center, is to stay inspired, enjoy and explore your inspiration, and trust that if an inspiration is yours to fulfill, the next right step to its fulfillment will show up in your world correctly according to the Strategy for your Type.

Bottom line? You don't have to figure things out!

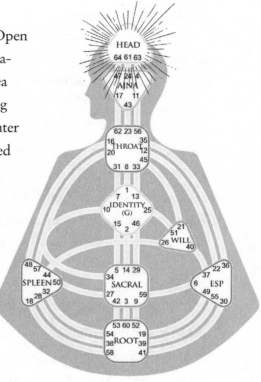

Figure 37: The Undefined Head Center.

Contemplation

- What truly inspires you?

- Do you give yourself time to cultivate inspiration? What do you need to do to stay inspired?

Affirmation

I am deeply inspired all the time. I am wise about what is truly inspiring. I follow my Strategy to help me decide what I need to do. The questions in my head are from others. I don't have to answer all of them—only the ones that truly excite me.

I am here to be wise about *managing my inspirations.*

Ajna Center Energy

The Ajna Center regulates concrete thinking. In the Ajna, we process information and inspiration, turning them into possibilities and potentially actionable thoughts. The Ajna is also where information, beliefs, and memories are stored.

Energy

If the Head Center is where we receive inspiration, the Ajna Center is where we translate those sparks of insight into action. Again, like with the Head Center, we are generating concrete possibilities, but we're not designed to then turn these possibilities into action. Time and awareness let us know when we can act on our ideas. Your beliefs and memories will influence how you translate inspiration into ideas.

Defined Ajna Center

When your Ajna Center is Defined, it will be green on your chart (see Figure 38). The Defined Ajna has the ability to hold on to fixed ideas and beliefs. If you have one, it means that you're also probably good at remembering things.

The Defined Ajna can be fixed or rigid in its way of thinking and can sometimes cause people to butt heads. Having a fixed way of thinking and the capacity to hold on to information is mostly a strength, though: it makes it easy to be certain about thoughts and ideas.

Challenge

When your Ajna Center is Defined, it's hard to see ideas from different angles, and you need help to perceive new perspectives and possibilities. It can be hard to change your mind when your Ajna is Defined, so making an effort to open your mind and really hear other people's viewpoints is essential to being more receptive to new ideas.

You can also sometimes have a hard time changing your mind if you have a negative mindset or self-limiting beliefs. You might need extra support and care as you work to instill new beliefs that are healthier and more self-loving.

Contemplation

- Do you consider yourself open-minded? What can you do to be more receptive to new ideas and the thoughts of others?

- Do you believe that you can be abundant, healthy, happy, and self-loving? Do you have beliefs that are encouraging and supportive? What are some ways you might cultivate a more loving and kinder self-image?

Affirmation

I am gentle with my thinking and always remember that there are many ways to think about information. I am uniquely capable of being certain. I listen carefully to the thoughts of others and allow for limitless thinking with grace.

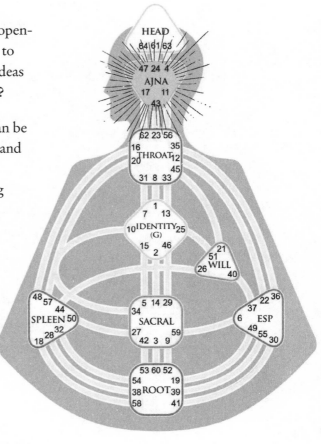

Figure 38: The Defined Anja.

I am here to be wise about *my thinking and capabilities.*

Undefined Ajna Center

If you have an Open Ajna, your gift is in being able to look at information, belief systems, and thoughts from multiple perspectives (see Figure 39). Your thoughts and ideas can be a great relief to other people, as they help expand what they view

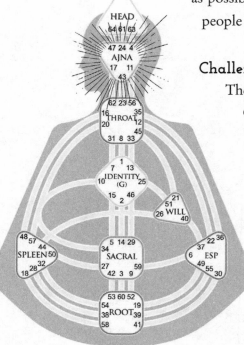

as possible in their lives. (This is especially true for people in your life with Defined Ajnas.)

Challenge

The challenge with having an Open Anja Center is allowing yourself that fluidity of perspective. We are conditioned to use our minds to figure things out and to be certain about what we know. Yet, we are meant to be open-minded. The purpose of the mind is to engage in *possibility*, not to determine absolute truth. If you're feeling pressure to hold on to a fixed idea or belief, give yourself some space and allow your thoughts to evolve and change.

Figure 39: The Undefined Anja.

Contemplation

- Do you feel pressured to be certain about things? Does making up your mind stress you out?

- Are you struggling to convince others (or even yourself) that you're certain?

- Do you wait to share your thoughts and opinions?

- How does it feel to play with the thoughts in your head versus trying to force them into a figurative box?

THE HUMAN DESIGN WORKBOOK

Affirmation

I am wise about information and beliefs. My gift is that I can see many sides of an issue and have many different understandings that are fluid and that change all the time. I don't have to make up my mind. I always write down the things I want to remember.

I am here to be wise about *information and perspectives.*

Throat Center Energy

The Throat Center carries the energy for communication as well as manifestation. In order to manifest what you want out in the world, you must be able to talk about it. The Throat Center helps to regulate the energy from the rest of your chart so that you can speak and initiate action in a way that will help you actualize our purpose.

Words create a template of possibility for action. When we put words to an idea, it starts the process of turning the idea into a reality. When you say to your partner that you'd like to go to a movie, the possibility of translating that idea into an evening of entertainment and fun is initiated by the conversation.

Interestingly, the Throat Center is physiologically associated with your thyroid and parathyroid glands, which play key roles in the regulation of growth and development. This means that when you do not use your Throat Center energy according to your Human Design, you not only go against the natural flow of energy, you also run the risk of burning out.

Think of it this way: if you are trying to push your ideas out into the world in the wrong way with the wrong people, you're going to try harder to get attention and recognition. This pushing can lead to a lifetime of trying to get attention—any attention—just to feel seen and heard. The correct use of Throat Center energy helps you learn how and when to communicate to others that your timing is right; you're valuing what you have to say enough to not say it to the wrong people; and you're not wasting your energy trying to get attention in the wrong way, at the wrong time, with people who don't value you.

Defined Throat Center

The Throat Center is the top square on the chart of your torso and will be brown if it's Defined (see Figure 40).

If your Throat Center is Defined, you're among the vast majority who have a consistent way of communicating and manifesting. The Gates and/or Channels your Throat is connected to will help you understand how to best use your energy for speaking and creating and tell you a lot about what you're designed to talk about with others. Two key aspects to using your Defined Throat Center are determined by whether or not your Throat Center is connected to a motor.

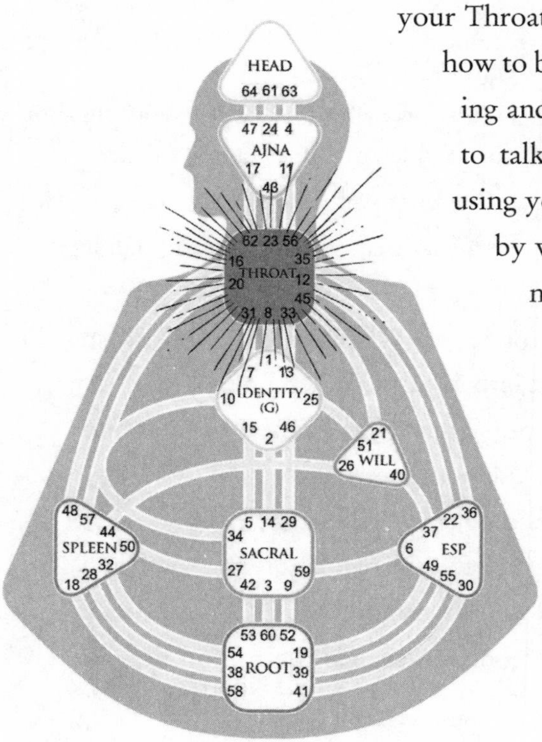

Figure 40: The Defined Throat Center.

Initiating versus Waiting

If your Throat Center is connected to a motorized Center—the Sacral, Will, Emotional Solar Plexus, or Root Center—then you either are a Manifestor or a Manifesting Generator, and you will be able to initiate conversation and action (see Figure 41). This means that you can strike up a conversation with someone at the grocery store or at the park. The key is to ensure that you're using your Strategy and Authority to help you determine when it's the right time and place to share.

If your Throat Center is connected to a non-motorized Center—the Ajna, G-Center, or Spleen—then you do best when you wait for recognition or an invitation to speak (see Figure 42). So, although you have a consistent way of

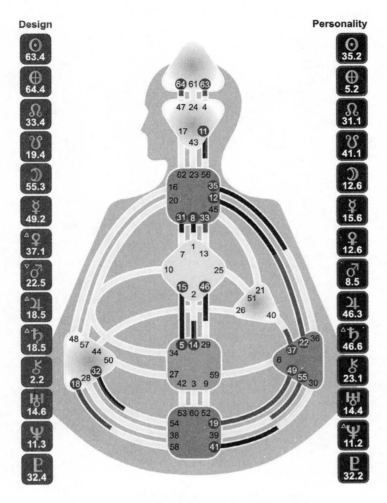

Figure 41: The motorized Throat Center.

communicating, you still need to wait until the timing is right to share. If you don't, you run the risk of feeling unheard or misunderstood, or of putting people off.

What You Talk About

What you're here to talk about will also be determined by what your Throat Center is connected to, so let's explore each of the Throat's possible connections:

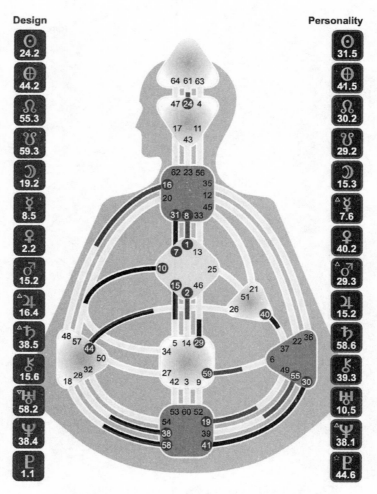

Design

24.2
44.2
55.3
59.3
19.2
8.5
2.2
15.2
16.4
38.5
15.6
58.2
38.4
1.1

Personality

31.5
41.5
30.2
29.2
15.3
7.6
40.2
29.3
15.2
58.6
39.3
10.5
38.1
44.6

Figure 42: The non-motorized Throat Center.

Ajna: You are able to speak your mind. Remember, this is a configuration that requires recognition or invitation. Think of how it feels when someone shares their opinion or beliefs without being asked. You want to make sure people are ready for your insights before you share.

Spleen: You can talk about your physicality and intuition. This is also a configuration that requires an invitation or recognition before sharing.

It can feel draining or quite sensitive sharing your physical issues or deep intuitive insights if the other person isn't ready for it.

G-Center: Everything you say comes straight from the depth of who you are. You are what you talk about. This is yet another configuration where you must be recognized or invited to speak before doing so, because sharing from such a sensitive place requires vulnerability. Criticism and judgment can be very painful for you, and it can potentially shut down your desire to share yourself with others. If this has happened to you, a life coach or supportive person might help you feel ready to share again.

Will: You will often speak with the pronoun "I" and talk about yourself—and that's okay! While many may think that people who talk about themselves are egotistical or self-important, and there is a possibility for that, there's also a potential for deep service. When you use your "I" to serve the community, this voice can be one of leadership and sustainability.

Emotional Solar Plexus: You can easily express your emotions, past and present.

Root: You can communicate about what drives you—what you're going to do, what you want to do, or what you can do.

Sacral: You can talk about your work as well as your relationships. Your communication and manifestation are directly linked to your life force energy. You are a Manifesting Generator.

Challenge

Knowing what you're here to talk about and when to share can help you communicate and manifest effectively. This is important, because even with a Defined Throat Center you can experience burnout if you don't use your energy properly. If you push when you should be waiting or wait when you should be pushing, you run the risk of burning out your thyroid/parathyroid—so be sure to take care of your voice. It's too precious to use without awareness.

Contemplation

- What are you meant to talk about and share with others?

- Do you feel comfortable with waiting for the right time to speak?

Affirmation

I speak with great responsibility and know the true spirit of my words. I allow others to have a voice, and I use my words to invite others to share.

I am here to be wise about *the spirit of words*.

Undefined Throat Center

If your Throat Center is Open, you have a natural ability to meet the needs of the people you're speaking with through your communication (see Figure 43). Openness gives you adaptability and fluidity. Your personal experience of all the different ways that people speak and share information gives you deep wisdom about how to best communicate. This also gives you an innate capacity to change the way you communicate, depending on who you're with.

Oprah is a great example of this energy in action. She has an Open Throat Center and uses it in her interviews to meet the needs of the interviewee, as well as when she's onstage, by becoming the voice of the room. People with Open Throat

Centers can also be excellent orators, singers, foreign language learners, and impressionists/ventriloquists.

If you're a leader or a teacher who has an Open Throat Center, you have the capacity to be a voice for your group or organization.

Challenge

The challenge with an Open Throat is often in feeling heard. Through your struggle with recognition and attention, you may repeatably talk without anyone really hearing you. When you're in a group setting, you may feel the pressure to speak without knowing what you're talking about. Or you may feel pressured to do something else to gain attention. If you've experienced any of these things, communication for you may be extremely painful. At times you may feel invisible, like no one is listening, or that you're misunderstood.

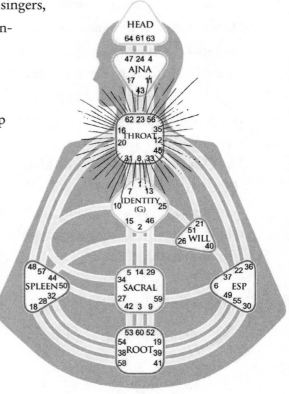

Figure 43: The Undefined Throat Center.

Although it may seem counterintuitive, Open Throat energy works best when you are silent and wait for someone to recognize or invite you to speak. In order for you to manifest and communicate properly, you need other people to instigate communication. It requires a trust in yourself and the right timing to wait in silence for someone to ask you to share something. This is especially true in Western society, where we are taught to voice our opinion and speak up.

However, when you wait in silence, you are cultivating a special wisdom. Once you receive recognition or an invitation, you know you're with people you can support through what you say and how you say it. Often, you'll receive feedback that whatever you shared was just what the other person needed to hear.

If you've been pushing through speaking or initiating without recognition, you may find yourself confronted with the thyroid/parathyroid issues mentioned earlier. You may also find that your voice becomes hoarse after using it this way. You also may feel like no one listens to you or that you can't communicate as effectively as other people. But what's true is that you have the capacity to be deeply influential and supportive through your communication when you wait for the right people to recognize your brilliance. So, start practicing silence and see what manifests.

Contemplation

- Are you trying to get attention—perhaps inappropriately—so that you can be heard?

- How does it feel to be silent? Are you willing to trust and value yourself enough to wait until people are ready for you to share your thoughts?

Affirmations

My words are heard best when I am invited to speak. I save my words for people who truly desire to hear my point of view and insights. I wait for the right people to ask me and value my words.

I am here to be wise about *communication and action.*

G-Center Energy

The G-Center carries the energy for love, direction, and the self. Everyone understands what it means to love and be loved, according to the Gates on the G-Center. (This is true whether your G-Center is Defined or not.)

Your alignment with love attunes the direction of your life and the expression of yourself.

You attract opportunities and experiences that become the direction your life is taking according to the energy of your G-Center. Furthermore, you can influence your life's direction and your sense of self by cultivating a greater love for yourself and others.

Defined G-Center

The diamond shape in the middle of the chart is the G-Center. It will be yellow if it is Defined (see Figure 44).

If your G-Center is Defined, which occurs in about 50 percent of the population, you will have a relatively fixed sense of yourself and your direction in life. Although you certainly grow and evolve, your core identity will remain consistent. No matter whether you're with your best friend or your boss, if you're at home or on vacation, or if Mercury is in retrograde, you are who you are. You can certainly be influenced by others in your life, but you won't take on their identity.

Your direction in life is also somewhat fixed. This doesn't mean you don't have choices — you most certainly do. Rather, it means that you're here to experience life in a certain way and that there

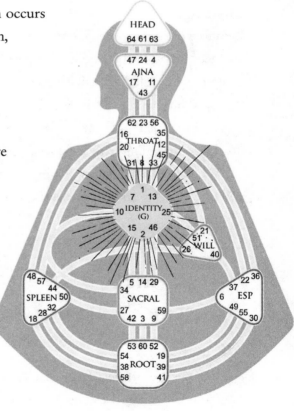

Figure 44: The Defined G-Center.

will be a little variability in that. You can experiment with experiences, but the essence of who you are and the direction you're going will remain the same. Think of it like this: if life is a mega buffet, when you have a Defined G-Center, it's like you can only order off the menu.

Often, people with a Defined G-Center are very comfortable and happy doing one thing (or a version of that thing) their whole lives—and that's totally okay. It can be quite freeing to realize that you are inherently on your path. You are then able to show up for the experiences in your life with an understanding that they are moving you forward in the direction your life is meant to take.

Challenge

Because your sense of self is consistent and fixed, it can be challenging to feel loved and accepted for who you are—especially if you are struggling with loving and accepting yourself. You will have a hard time not being authentic, so it's important that you value and love who you are. Working with a trained Human Design specialist or other support person can help you shift your relationship with yourself if you are struggling with self-love or self-acceptance.

When you build a deep, loving relationship with yourself, your sense of self will be more aligned, and your life direction will unfold accordingly.

Contemplation

- Do you love and accept yourself? What do you love about yourself?

- What have your life experiences taught you about yourself?

Affirmation

I am who I am. I express myself in all that I do. I celebrate the magnificence of who I am.

I am here to be wise about *expression of the self.*

Undefined G-Center

If you have an Open G-Center, there is malleability and variability to your experience of love, direction, and self-identity (see Figure 45). You take in and amplify these energies from other people—their life experiences, their wounds and pains, their sense of self, their lovability and worthiness. You are incredibly sensitive to others!

Challenge

Your sensitivity can translate into questioning your lovability and authenticity. You may feel like others don't understand you, or that you are inauthentic because you act differently depending on which person you are with. It can be difficult to know which identity is yours among the many you encounter throughout your life.

You may also feel like you merge with the people you are in relationships with because you experience them so deeply. This is especially tricky because you are easily able to see the potential in people and fall in love with nearly everyone you meet. It's important for you to set good boundaries and to choose your relationships based on what someone actually does versus the potential you might see in them.

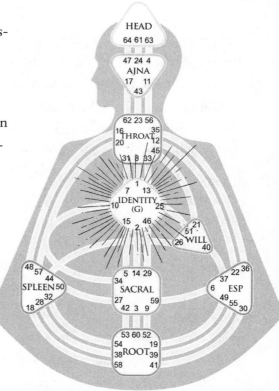

Figure 45: The Undefined G-Center.

When it comes to your life's direction, you may feel overwhelmed and that you're lacking clarity because there's so much variability in your life path. People with an Open G-Center often feel like they can't find their life purpose or struggle to know which path to take. The important thing to remember is that it doesn't matter so much the direction you take; rather, it's about what you learn from whichever direction you choose. Freedom is available in the abundance of options.

When you have an Open G-Center, you learn about life and your life path by sampling many different options. Eventually, you learn what you like and what feels most like you from your experience. When you understand what you like, you begin to define for yourself what it means to be at peace with who you are.

One of the crucial aspects to managing these sensitivities is finding the right environment and the right people for you. When you are in the wrong environment, it can create tension in every area of your life. You might feel like you're dating all the wrong people, that opportunities for growth are scarce, or that your momentum has come to a standstill. These feelings are your inner compass. If you feel stuck, make sure your physical environment feels good—everything from the placement of your bed in your room to your city and country.

If your environment feels off, you've outgrown the place you're at and it's time to change it. By changing where you live, where your desk is located, and/ or the people you're surrounding yourself with, you adjust your life direction and sense of self. Making a big change in your physical environment, according to your Type and Strategy, can be a game changer because it opens you up to opportunities, experiences, and people that are supportive of your life path.

When you are in the right environment, your wisdom about love, identity, and direction can be more easily expressed because you are amplifying the aligned values and integrity around you. When you learn to love yourself, regardless of how you show up that day, you are living out the highest expression of this energy. When you learn the lessons of how to be at home with yourself and how to love yourself—even the parts that seem fluid and changeable—you'll be able to offer the priceless gift of self-love and self-acceptance to others, helping them feel seen and loved for who they truly are.

Contemplation

- Is your current environment lifting you up, or is it time for you to make a change?

- Do you feel lovable and seen by the people you're with? Do the people you're with reflect the same values as you?

Affirmation

How I experience myself changes depending on those around me. Therefore, I choose to surround myself with people who feel good to me. Place is very important to me, and I create an environment that's soothing. When I am in the right place, the right opportunities come to me.

I am here to be wise about *love, authenticity, and direction.*

Will Center Energy

The Will Center is where we experience the physical manifestation of turning value into form. This is the Center that regulates the energy of money, possessions, resources, and commerce. It is a very material Energy Center that lends itself to measuring value with things and numbers. In the shadow of this energy, we take our value from how much money we have or how many possessions we own.

One way to understand these energies and how they work together is through the concept of endurance. In order to keep generating resources and material goods, we need to have sustainable energy. To have sustainable energy, we must rest. In order to rest, we must believe that our contribution to the world is so valuable that we are worthy of resting enough to sustain it. Any disruption in this cycle, and we find ourselves pushing with energy we don't have and potentially burning out.

I want to highlight something about the Will Center, which is that it operates through cycles. Therefore, we can manifest on a physical plane, but we won't have the energy to keep manifesting if we don't regularly stop and resource ourselves by pausing and doing something purely for relaxation and rest.

Interestingly, there is also mysticism in this Center, which helps us to better understand the ego. By nature, we each have a differentiated ego (or human self), and this differentiation says, "I'm part of the puzzle and I have to do my part very well to be of service to the greater good." And so, we are meant to surrender our ego and use our uniqueness as a foundation for service toward the well-being of others. This may look like supporting people financially and materially, as well as through other resources like teaching or providing clean water and air. When we surrender the energies of the Will Center—such as money, things of value, the ego, personal willpower, etc.—to something greater than ourselves, we allow our individual lives to serve the betterment of others.

Defined Will Center

The Will Center is the smaller triangle just to the right of the diamond-shaped G-Center (see Figure 46). Your Will Center will be red if it's Defined. Only a few people—only about 12 percent of the population—have this Center Defined.

If you have a Defined Will Center, you have consistent access to willpower and, as such, you must learn to "work to rest." To use this energy wisely and sustainably, you must listen to your need for cycles of rest. Because you have access to willpower, you may find yourself pushing through the desire to take a break. But if you do this enough, you'll burn yourself out and potentially crash your immune or digestive system.

You are here to empower others. This can be through teaching, sharing resources, or sharing your experience or viewpoint. You may notice that you tend to speak using the pronoun "I." This is part of the ego aspect of the Will Center— you are designed to talk about yourself. This is not meant to be egotistical; rather, it is about speaking from your personal ego as a way of being of service to others. It requires both listening and surrender.

You are here to bring things into the material plane. While that can certainly translate into money, it can also look like creating other resources of value, such as food, shelter, and information. You may be very connected to material things and take good care of the things you have—or even love your things. For many on a spiritual path, it can feel uncomfortable to have such a relationship with the energy surrounding ego, money, and material things.

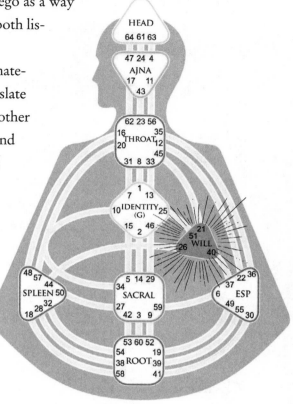

Figure 46: The Defined Will Center.

Challenge

The first thing I always ask people with a Defined Will Center is whether or not they are getting enough rest. It's important to note that this rest needs to be truly off—this isn't about relaxing in a hammock listening to self-help books on audio or mentally revisiting your finances. You are designed to rest, and therefore you must really rest. If you're not getting enough rest, get curious about why that is. In order to truly rest, you must believe you are worthy of it.

When you remember that you are here to surrender your unique human expression to being of service, you will naturally use your life and your resources to empower others.

Contemplation

- Are you getting enough rest? Do you value yourself enough to take time off and recharge?

- How are you using your life in the service of others?

Affirmation

It is important for me to rest. Rest allows me to recharge my willpower. I honor the promises that I make and understand that people expect me to keep my promises. I am gentle with my expectations of others. Not everyone can do the things that I do.

I am here to be wise about *measuring value and empowering others.*

Undefined Will Center

If you have an Open Will Center, you're here to become wise about what's truly valuable in life (see Figure 47). You will discover that it is not about material things at all!

Challenge

The biggest theme of the Open Will Center is in questioning your own value. Self-worth lives in this part of the chart, and there can be a drive to prove yourself here. You may feel terrified that you have no value or feel like you're not being valued in a relationship or other part of your life. You may also find you undervalue your contribution to something or even your work as a whole. For example, people in the service industry often undervalue their services and don't charge what they're really worth.

You may also find you have a tendency to override your need for rest. We live in a society that is obsessed with working harder in order to achieve better results—despite the fact that most of us don't have the ability to maintain this frenetic pace. You can get tied up in this idea that if you just keep working, you'll eventually prove how good, strong, capable, intelligent, or otherwise valuable you are. Yet, what's true is that you are inherently valuable and worthy. And when you live from this place, you recognize your need for rest and value yourself enough to take it. When you do rest, your ability to offer your value to others increases.

You are, in fact, so valuable that you must take care of yourself so you can do a better job of expanding, growing, and helping to evolve the world. You are worthy of a savings account, charging enough for your services, and restoring your energy because you are a more brilliant version of yourself when you do.

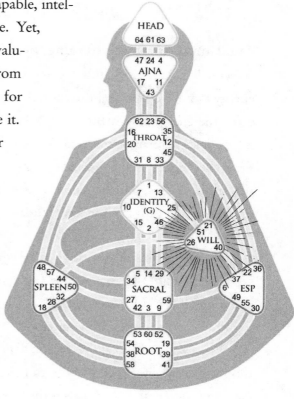

Figure 47: The Undefined Will Center.

Contemplation

- Is there anything you're trying to prove?

- Do you believe in your inherent worthiness and value?

- Are you getting enough rest?

Affirmation

I enter into all agreements according to my Human Design Strategy. I make promises and commitments carefully and deliberately. I have nothing to prove, and I value myself deeply. I fearlessly ask to be paid what I am worth.

I am here to be wise about *self-worth and value.*

Emotional Solar Plexus Energy

As you likely guessed, this Center is all about emotions—the frequencies of energy that have a natural flow and fluidity about them. It's the place where you carry the energy that makes you human. No other animal has the capacity for intentional creativity in the same way humans do. This Center is responsible for all the archetypes that we associate with creativity, such as romance, passion, poetry, sex, spiritual bliss, intimacy, imagination, relationship with nature and the divine order, and the capacity for new human experiences—and, in the shadows, war, chaos, and melancholy.

It is the nature of emotions that they come and go. Luckily, you have the capacity to shift and change this frequency of energy through your focus and attention. The most important piece to understand is that you have the capacity to influence and work with your emotional energy with the power of your mind.

When you learn to allow, accept, and embrace both the highs and the lows of this inherent wave of energy, you can choose to create with purpose. Where you place your focus and awareness is the modulator of this process.

For example, if you're feeling sad, you might ask yourself, *What's wrong with me?* You might think, *I'm worthless; I made a huge mistake,* or focus on how terrible you're feeling. Each of those thought processes takes your attention to lower vibrations. In other words, you begin to feel sadder for longer time periods. On the other hand, if you are feeling deep sadness and recognize it as a sign to nurture yourself, go deep within, and trust in the underlying abundance and goodness of life, you will find that the amount of time you spend in sadness decreases.

Knowing how this Center is configured in your chart can help you regulate your emotional energy and learn how to use it become more intentional and pro-active instead of reactive.

Defined Emotional Solar Plexus Center

The Emotional Solar Plexus (ESP) Center is the triangle on the far right side of your chart (see Figure 48). Yours will be brown if it's Defined. Half the population has a Defined ESP.

If you have a Defined Emotional Solar Plexus, it's in your nature to experience your life emotionally through cycles or waves. You're designed to have inner cycles of contemplation, integration, and creative expression (often experienced as the low point in your wave), as well as outer, more expressive cycles of creativity, sharing what you know and expressing what you've felt or experienced (often the high point of your wave). You'll have emotions that feel good, inspired, joyful, and hopeful, and cycles where you may feel melancholic and introspective. It's important to remember that no emotional energies are good or bad, though some may feel quite unpleasant. Each plays a role in your experience of life and your expression of who you are.

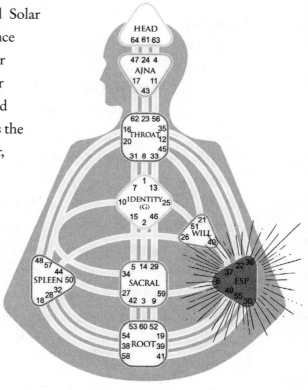

Figure 48: The Defined Emotional Solar Plexus.

Your emotional energy isn't different from any other physiological rhythm, such as a circadian rhythm or a menstrual cycle. Your wavelike emotionality is inherent to your nature. Therefore, the best way to work with this energy is to allow it to be, just like your need for rest.

The best things to do when you're experiencing the low end of your wave are to notice it and accept it, keeping in mind that this is not a permanent state. This keeps you from feeling trapped in the low expression of your emotional energy.

Challenge

Remember that your wave is a natural part of who you are and there is nothing in your environment or your mind that is causing the low or high end of your wave. Allowing the melancholy will enable you to use this energy to your creative advantage, take better care of yourself, and open yourself to new possibilities moving forward. Melancholy is a time of inward reflection, rest, and renewal. It's important to let yourself slow down, so you can enjoy time of contemplation or creative thought when you're low on your wave.

My husband is an architect with a lot of emotional Definition. He's a wildly creative person. When he experiences the low end of his wave, he savors the melancholy. Melancholy is a profoundly creative state for him. When he's melancholic, he likes to listen to the blues, staying up late after everyone has gone to bed and spending hours drawing by hand and writing notes in his journal related to design and the future of the world. It helps him process all his creative inspirations and better present them to his design students or colleagues.

You are not a victim of your emotional wave. You will always have emotional energy, and it's yours to use in a way that supports your creativity, self-care, and self-expression.

If you are interested in understanding your wave better, I highly encourage you to track your emotional wave daily over three months or so, then look for patterns. Some people find that their emotions are quite predictable and rhythmic, while others find less of a pattern but can connect more with their internal state following this practice. Either way, I encourage experimentation as a first step in more consciously utilizing your creative emotional energy.

Contemplation

- How do you treat yourself when you're low on your emotional wave?

- Do you have ways of taking care of yourself that enable you to access your creativity when you're feeling low? What are your creative outlets?

Affirmation

I take my time making decisions and know that I reach clarity over time. I am here to be deliberate, not spontaneous.

I am here to be wise about *emotional cycles and waves.*

Undefined Emotional Solar Plexus Center

If your Emotional Solar Plexus is Open, you are empathic and here to be wise about emotional energy (see Figure 49). You feel other people's emotional energy deeply—often more deeply than they do themselves—because you take it in and amplify it.

Challenge

Because everyone tends to judge emotions and because it can be intense to feel amplified emotions, you may find yourself trying to avoid them altogether. This can result in a tendency to "make nice" or trying not to "make waves" with the people in your life. You may find you have a hard time speaking up for yourself or stating your beliefs, simply because you don't want to upset anyone. Conversely, you may have a sort of addiction to dramatic energy, especially if you grew up in a family with a lot of emotional Definition.

Of course, if you learn to make nice, please people, and avoid handling conflict or difficult conversations, you will inevitably find that your own boundaries get crossed (or maybe you haven't even been able to establish them in the first place).

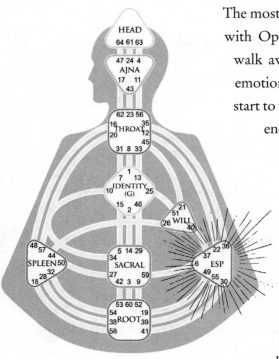

Figure 49: The Undefined
Emotional Solar Plexus.

The most effective Strategy I recommend for people with Open Emotional Solar Plexus Centers is to walk away from a person or situation when the emotional energy becomes too intense. When you start to feel overwhelmed, it's time to get out of the energy field you share with the other person/people and move to a place where you can be alone. You'll find it only takes about fifteen minutes before you begin to decompress.

It can also be helpful to remind yourself of the inherent nature of the emotional wave. Then you can begin to depersonalize your amplified experience of another person's emotion and make peace with speaking your truth or setting a boundary even when emotions are running high. Learning to be in the middle of a deeply emotional situation while not reacting to the energy is the biggest challenge in cultivating the wisdom of this Open Center.

In essence, when you have an Open Emotional Solar Plexus, you have to learn to be an emotional screen, allowing the experience of other people's emotions flow through you, instead of being a sponge, absorbing the feelings of others and feeling responsible for them or identifying with them. The minute you learn to see this for what it is and stop identifying with and reacting to other people's emotions, is the minute you begin to break old patterns of trying to take care of other people at cost to your own emotional state.

Remember: you experience emotions and feelings, but they are not who you are. When you find yourself identifying with the emotional energy, you begin to hold on to it and may even feel like it's yours to fix. Many of you may be holding onto a lifetime of other people's emotional energy because you didn't understand the mechanics of emotions.

The saying I love to share with people is, "Be a screen and not a sponge." In other words, allow emotional energy to move through you; increase your capacity for empathy, compassion, and creativity; and then watch it pass. If you're struggling with holding what may be a lifetime of other people's emotions, I encourage you to seek support in processing it. In my own work, I have seen the tremendous benefits of Emotionally Focused Therapy (EFT) and the Quantum Alignment System™, but there are many others as well. (To learn more, visit https://karen-curryparker.teachable.com/p/deconditioningbydesign.) No matter the avenue, I hope you give yourself the gift of releasing the emotional energy that was never yours to carry.

Contemplation

- Are you avoiding truth and conflict?

- Are you trying to keep everyone happy?

Affirmation

I can make decisions in the moment. I pay attention to the spirit of my emotions and allow others to experience their feelings without making their experience my own. I am very sensitive, and I trust my insights about other people's feelings. I take frequent breaks when the emotional energy is too intense.

I am here to be wise about *emotions.*

Sacral Center Energy

The Sacral Center contains the most powerful energy in the chart: life force and workforce energy. What I mean by life force and workforce energy is anything that's required to bring a person into the world, raise them through adulthood, and care for the family/community. This includes sex, the energy to care for and feed a baby, providing resources for a child, working to provide for yourself and your family, and transmitting the values of the family/community to its members.

You'll recall from Chapter 2 that whether or not your Sacral Center is Defined is a major factor in determining your Type, so you'll gain a greater understanding of this Center by comparing the concepts we explored there with the ones here.

The key to understanding how the energy of this Center works is through the concept of sustainability. The Sacral Center is a powerhouse for the life force and workforce that keeps going and going when it's Defined. There are, of course, ways to keep yourself sustainable and in the flow of your right energy whether your Sacral Center is Defined or Open—that's what we'll explore here.

Defined Sacral Center

The Sacral Center is the square in the middle of the chart (see Figure 50). Yours will be red if it's Defined. About 70 percent of people have a Defined Sacral Center.

Much of what you need to know about having a Defined Sacral Center is in the description of your Type in Chapter 2. In this chapter, I want to expand on the importance of responding to the right work and leveraging your energy as it relates to this Center.

When it comes to utilizing the power of your Sacral Center in the most optimal way, it is crucial that you respond to the right work and the right relationships. As we discussed in Chapter 2, the way to access the knowing of yourself available in the Sacral Center is through the Sacral sounds.

In responding to the Sacral sounds of *uh-huh* and *uhn-uh*, you tap into a treasure trove of all things related to life force and workforce energy. You may even find you have a need for less sleep because your energy is sustainable. Note: it can be hard to stop this energy once it's turned on because it feels so good.

Challenge

Just because Sacral Center energy is sustainable doesn't mean you can't experience burnout or other forms of energy depletion. For example, if you really hate your job, you may still force yourself to show up every day because you have sustainable workforce energy available to you. In this case, your energy does have a quality of sustainability to it, but you will eventually experience burnout because you're not aligned with the right work. Interestingly, you'll find that often when you do quit work that isn't right for you according to your Type and Strategy and begin work that is aligned, your energy will bounce back quite quickly. By using your Sacral response, you'll stay connected with right work and right relationships and be able to leverage your energy to do the work that's aligned with your purpose.

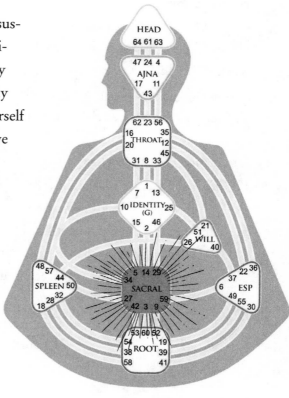

Figure 50: The Defined Sacral Center.

Contemplation

- Are you doing your right work?

- Are you using your sustainable energy to keep you going in a job or relationship that isn't right for you?

Affirmation

I wait with grace and patience, knowing that the right opportunities will show up for me. All I have to do is respond to the world and I will joyfully do the right work and be with the right people. I fearlessly honor my response and know that I am internally driven to be in the right place at the right time, doing the right work.

I am here to be wise about *responding.*

Undefined Sacral Center

If your Sacral Center is Open, the most important thing to understand is that the quality of your life force and workforce energy will not be sustainable (see Figure 51). This means that even something like raising a child or working a nine-to-five will eventually burn you out if you don't have sufficient downtime and support.

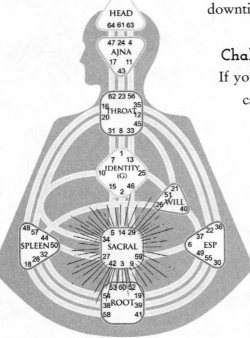

Figure 51: The Undefined Sacral Center.

Challenge

If your Sacral Center is Open, in the short run it can seem like you've got way more energy than most people. You can likely think of times in your life when you worked harder, got more done, or otherwise used your energy in a way that defied what others were capable of. This is because you've borrowed Defined Sacral Center energy from someone through the amplification process. It's crucial to recognize that this energy isn't yours, and it isn't sustainable. You are designed to be energized and to have access to energy in the short run, but you have to allow yourself to rest, reset, and renew your energy on a regular basis.

As a result of this energy dynamic, it's common to not know when enough is enough. If you're doing thirty times more work than everyone else (and likely getting accolades for it) but don't realize you're running on energy that isn't yours, you may continue to push yourself despite the fact that your body, mind, and spirit are trying to tell you that you've had enough. You may also fear being seen as lazy, so you overcompensate by working more than everyone else. If you keep pushing, at a certain point you'll crash and burn, and you'll potentially not understand where all your energy went and what is "wrong" with you.

This is often how this theme plays out in work, but you can also see how it could show up in relationships as well (for example, in overcaring, overgiving, pushing past self-care, etc.). And sadly, the burnout from pushing with this borrowed energy for too long can result in serious exhaustion on a physical level, which can take a long time to recover from.

The flip side of this is a deep wisdom about the energy that people use in their work and in their personal lives. Often, people with Open Sacral Centers are quite satisfied in a job that highlights skills for helping people manage their energy effectively, such as being managers, coaches, or therapists. You'll have an innate sense about how other people use their life force energy and can help them guide and manage it according to your Type and Strategy.

An element of trust is necessary for working with this energy in its highest expression, because its nature counters our ideas of how to become successful in work and in life. When you give yourself the rest you need and begin to follow your Type and Strategy, you will find that your wisdom and value have far reaches and are far more sustainable than the forced work you've tried in your past. As you work to decondition your pattern of pushing with energy that isn't yours and relax into the flow of energy that's there for you, you may eventually find that you can intentionally harness your Sacral energy and use it to your advantage in short spurts.

Contemplation

- Do you know when enough is enough?

- Are you getting enough downtime, support, and rest?

Affirmation

I am not here to work in the traditional way. I can work hard in short bursts, and then I need alone time to discharge the extra energy I carry. I recognize that my energy is mutable, and I take care of myself and let go of the expectations of others. I am very powerful when I am using my energy correctly.

I am here to be wise about *life force and work force energy.*

Spleen Center Energy

The Spleen Center gives you intuitive pulses that help you know when to take action. It also gives you a gut feeling about what you need to do to preserve your health and well-being. You may be wondering how each of these seemingly dissimilar themes are related. It can be helpful to begin with the concept of instinct, which is essential for survival. When we hear a sound that doesn't feel safe, go into a dark alley at night, or even decide to throw out food from the fridge that seems off, we are accessing our instinctual sense. It's all focused on helping us stay alive.

We have an energetic, instinctive capacity that can be thought of as a survival drive. It is a direct, reactive response in the moment to a situation or circumstance. In that moment, we take action—fight or flight—to keep us alive. Health comes in as another key aspect of survival—instinctually, we are driven to maintain our health to keep ourselves alive. So, we kick into action when we are in danger and need to make a certain choice in the moment to protect ourselves.

We all have this survival instinct, and it is an important aspect of keeping us safe when real danger arises. However, I'm sure you can easily come up with some situations in your life when you felt extremely afraid, despite the situation actually being quite benign. This is because we are complex beings with consciousness, emotions, inspirations, drivers around lovability and worthiness, etc. So, instead of only feeling afraid when our safety is threatened, we also are afraid of moving to a new city, writing a book, saying "I love you" in a romantic relationship, or even changing careers.

Whether your Spleen Center is Defined or Open, you're vulnerable to experiencing these fears. The good news is that the solution to working with them is simple: feel the fear and do it anyway. This isn't always easy, because the experience of fear is hardwired. We can literally feel like we are about to die before giving a big speech if we have a deep, unquestioned fear of being inadequate and failing, for example. It can feel completely unnatural to walk up onto stage when you're terrified, but remember that this energy is limited. Taking action will break through this fear, and when you get to the other side, you will notice how hard it is to reconnect with those same fears again. You'll be creating a new, more courageous narrative, and your neural networks will begin to rewire.

Defined Spleen Center

You can find the Spleen Center on the far left side of the Human Design chart (see Figure 52). It's shaped like a triangle and will be brown if it is Defined.

If you have a Defined Spleen Center, you will have a consistent experience of time, intuition, health, and survival. Your inner sense of time is deep, and you may be able to tell what time it is without looking at the clock. Your experience of your intuition is likely consistent as well. There are many ways to experience intuition, including clairaudience (hearing), clairvoyance (seeing), claircognizance (knowing), clairsentience (sensing), clairolfactance (smelling), and dreaming. So, whichever way you get your extrasensory knowing, it's likely your consistent way of accessing your intuition.

You also have a fixed, insensitive immune system. This means that by the time you realize you're coming down with something, you're quite sick and may need

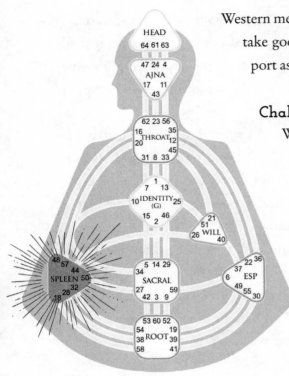

HEAD
64 61 63

47 24 4
AJNA
17 11
43

62 23 56
16   35
    THROAT 12
20   45
31 8 33

1   13
10 IDENTITY 25
   (G)
15   46
   2
26 WILL 40
   21
   51

5 14 29
34
SACRAL
27   59
42 3 9

48
57 44
SPLEEN 50
28 32
18

37 22 36
6   ESP
49 55 30

53 60 52
54   19
38 ROOT 39
58   41

Figure 52: The Defined Spleen Center.

Western medicine to help you recover. So, make sure to take good care of your physical body and get support as soon as you start feeling under the weather.

Challenge

When it comes to the fears of the Spleen Center, you may find yourself grounded in one or more of them. It can feel like you've lost momentum and enthusiasm. With a Defined Spleen Center, you'll find that moving through these fears by taking intentional action breaks the fear's hold and moves you into courage.

Contemplation

- What fears are holding you back from taking action in your life?

- Are you taking good care of your physical body?

- Are you trusting your intuition?

Affirmation

I trust my intuition. I listen to my gut feelings and take guided action. I listen to my body. I rest and take care of myself. I honor my sense of time. I remember that not everyone is as fast as me, and I flow with universal timing.

I am here to be wise about *trusting my gut feelings.*

Undefined Spleen Center

If your Spleen Center is Open, you have a fluid sense of time and timing, intuition, health, and survival (see Figure 53). Your relationship with the time-space continuum is flexible, which means you may lose your connection to linear time. You may find yourself overcompensating for this by either becoming hypervigilant about being early or chronically late to appointments. In its highest expression, your lack of connection with time can be experienced as an engagement in the flow of life when you pay attention within the present moment.

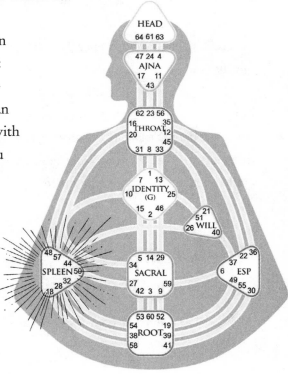

Figure 53: The Undefined Spleen Center.

Although many people with an Open Spleen Center report that they don't feel very intuitive, the opposite is actually true. You have the potential for an amplified intuitive ability that comes with an inherent variability, meaning, you may experience your intuition through clear-sightedness, auditory signals, a felt sense, smells, and through your dreams—all depending on where you are, who you're with, and the cosmic weather at the time. The key here is to trust in your various ways of knowing—it is a gift!

In addition to your intuitive sense, your immune system is also quite sensitive. You probably have noticed that you can tell when you're getting sick before the traditional symptoms begin to show themselves. You have a deeper attunement to what's going on with your physical body, so you're aware when things shift. You may also pick up on other people's health and wellness and even experience it in your own body. Many people with an Open Spleen Center are medically empathic or intuitive. As a result of this sensitivity, you'll find you do best with alternative, gentler methods of healing and medication.

Challenge

When it comes to health and survival, the Open Spleen Center carries a desire to hold on to things to stay safe, happy, and secure. This can be anything—your job or relationships, the poem from your first boyfriend, old stories or emotions. There's an unconscious energetic drive that says, *Better hold on, I might need this for my survival!*

So, if you're feeling unhappy in your career, relationship, or even just with a lot of stuff, whether physical or energetic, try asking yourself, *Am I holding on to this for longer than I should?* If the answer is yes, remember that although you'll feel the fears of this Center more intensely, the guidance from earlier is just as powerful and effective: try identifying the fear(s) that keep you holding on, then do—or get rid of—whatever it is anyway.

Contemplation

- How well do you take care of your physical body?

- Do you trust your intuition even if it shows up in different ways?

- Are you holding on to things, people, or pain for longer than is good for you? If so, do you know what you're afraid of losing?

Affirmation

I easily let go of all things that do not serve my highest good. I honor my body and the messages it sends me. When I feel sick, I rest. I honor my own sense of timing and know that whenever I arrive is just perfect. I respect other people's sense of time and always wear a watch. I trust my intuition and know that I receive intuitive insights in many ways.

I am here to be wise about *intuition and timing.*

Root Center Energy

The Root Center is the Center for adrenaline—a driver that helps us get things done. It's the get-up-and-go behind doing what needs to be done to be self-actualized, take action, or create. It is also a pressure Center like the Head Center, and as such, it carries a certain amount of stress energy. When our adrenaline is high and we feel pressure to get things done, it can bring on a certain amount of stress.

Defined Root Center

The Root Center is the square at the bottom of the Human Design chart (see Figure 54). It will be brown if it's Defined. About half the population has a Defined Root Center.

If your Root Center is Defined, you'll notice that you have a consistent pressure to get things done. However, you may not always feel "on" and ready to knock out your next project, because this energy operates in a pulse that turns on and off.

You'll know your energy is turned on when things feel right, the timing is right, and/or when it is time to act. When any of those three

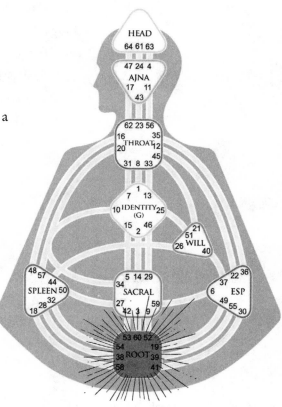

Figure 54: The Defined Root Center.

components are out of alignment, your energy to get things done will be turned off.

When your Root Center is Defined, what you're motivated to do depends on what other Center is connected to it. If you look at your Root Center, you'll find a colored line (in black, red, or both) that connects it to the Sacral Center, the Emotional Solar Plexus, and/or the Spleen.

Defined Root Center and Sacral Center

If your Root Center is connected to the Sacral Center, the Root pulse to get things done acts as an on/off switch for your Sacral energies (see Figure 55). This means that when your Root Center pulse is on, you'll feel an enormous drive to get things done and you can manifest things in a powerful way. When your Root Center pulse is off, you can feel completely drained of energy, both physically and mentally. It's like you can't get your mojo going, making it can feel nearly impossible to accomplish things.

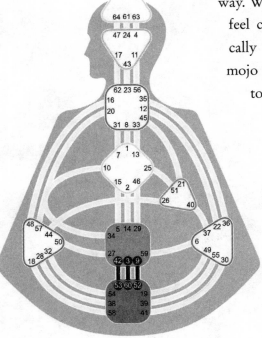

Figure 55: The Defined Root Center is connected to the Defined Sacral Center.

Challenge

When you start to feel into these energies, you will notice that often your Root Center pulse is aiding you in determining when the timing is right to take an action. When the energy isn't there, the pulse is off, so it's time to stop pushing or trying to make something happen. Instead of seeing this as procrastination, try exploring whether or not it actually might be about trusting in the right timing.

You'll know when the timing is right when life presents you an opportunity that syncs with your Strategy and Authority for your Type.

For example, you might feel pressure to start a business. The more you think about it, the more pressure you might experience to get started. If you follow that pressure without the internal alignment (Manifestor), something to respond to (Generator or Manifesting Generator), an invitation (Projector), or clarity (Reflector), you might just be reacting to the pressure and not actually starting the business that is yours to start.

Defined Root Center and Emotional Solar Plexus

If your Root Center and your Emotional Solar Plexus are connected (see Figure 56), you'll notice that when your mood goes down (i.e., you're at a low point on your emotional wave), your adrenaline drops as well. Often the first sign is that you start to become sluggish.

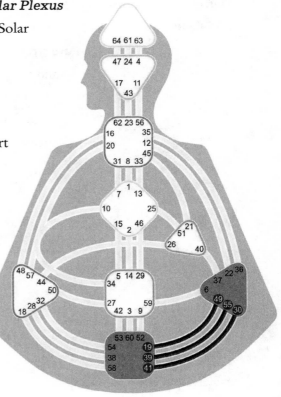

One of the best ways to work with this energy is to make sure you're giving yourself plenty of time to ride your emotional wave before you make a decision (see Chapter 2). If you don't wait for clarity, you may find yourself committed to something that you don't have the energy to carry out, because your Root Center pulse turns off when you reach the low point of your

Figure 56: The Defined Root Center is connected to the Defined Emotional Solar Plexus.

wave. Understandably, this can lead to feeling like a failure or like you can never follow through, when it's really just a matter of energy mechanics.

Challenge

The challenge is learning to allow yourself the time to make decisions and not taking the occasional lack in energy personally. Using the strategies in the section on the Emotional Solar Plexus can help you with what to do when your mood and your motivation are low.

Defined Root Center and Spleen Center

If your Root Center is connected to your Spleen Center (see Figure 57), you will more strongly experience the connection between drive and timing. When the timing isn't right to do something, your adrenaline pulse will turn off. If you can gauge your own energy around motivation, drive, and the physical energy to get something done, you will begin to gain insight into right timing. In other words, if you don't feel like it, assess whether you're actually procrastinating or whether you are sensing that that timing is not quite right.

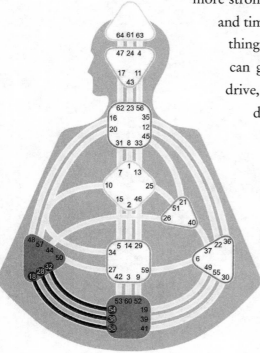

Figure 57: The Defined Root Center is connected to the Defined Spleen Center.

Challenge

If you can't seem to motivate yourself to do something, it's very likely it's because the timing isn't right. Learning to trust yourself and your adrenaline energy is a key to using this energy wisely.

Contemplation

- How do you use your energy to get things done?

- Do you take care of yourself when your energy feels low?

Affirmation

I honor my Root pulse and wait for the energy to get things done. I get more done when that energy pulse is on. When the energy is off, I know that it is my time to rest and restore.

I am here to be wise about *gauging my energy levels and rest.*

Undefined Root Center

If your Root Center is Open, you will experience a constant pressure to get things done (see Figure 58). This is because you're taking in the adrenaline energy of the people around you and amplifying it.

Challenge

You probably have a never-ending, ever-expanding to-do list that keeps your energy occupied—if not physically, at least mentally. You may also feel like if you can just get this one thing done, then you'll be free to get/do/be XYZ. Yet as soon as you finish one thing, there is another always waiting in the wings. This can translate to never taking a break, rushing through things just to be done with them, or procrastinating.

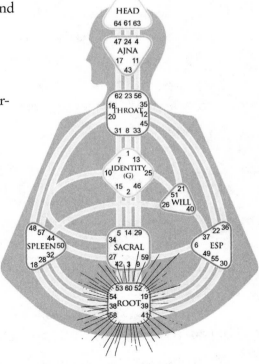

Figure 58: The Undefined Root Center.

The energy of this Open Center will place pressure on everything else in your chart. So you may find yourself feeling pressured to give someone something in order to feel lovable or worthy. Or you might feel pressured to share your thoughts in order to be heard and seen or pressured to keep working when your body, mind, and spirit are asking for a break.

This plays out quite interestingly in relationship dynamics. A person with a Defined Root Center will be exuding adrenaline pressure energy all the time, no matter what they say or do. It's not personal, however. But when you engage in any way with someone with a Defined Root Center, you can feel like they are pressuring you to get something done.

For example, your partner may ask, "Would you like some coffee?" and it can feel like they are wanting you to go into the kitchen to start the coffeepot, when they genuinely only want to know if you want coffee. Of course, when you're in conversation about division of household labor, childcare, or a deadline for a project, you can see how this energy could feel much more intense.

This dynamic can lead to agreeing to something because of the pressure you feel to say yes. This pressure can also fuel a love for being onstage or engaging in risky behaviors/activities or a complete avoidance of them because the pressure is too much.

We live in a society addicted to this adrenaline pressure. Our drive to do-do-do and get things done is fueled by coffee, energy drinks, and the like.

One of the best ways to work with this energy is to first bring awareness to it. When you can recognize the energy dynamics at play, you start to see that often the pressure you're perceiving from your partner, boss, kids, or colleagues is purely energetic. In other words, they don't actually want, need, or expect you to do anything.

Once that awareness begins to soften the energy, you can ask yourself this follow-up question: What's the worst thing that could happen if I don't do this? More often than not, the answer is nothing. And if you don't wait until the last minute to get something done, you'll give yourself plenty of time to work with the pressure and give yourself the space and time you need to move forward.

Contemplation

- Are you rushing to get things done so you can be free or procrastinating because you feel overwhelmed by all the things on your list?

- What's the worst thing that might happen if you don't complete everything on your to-do list?

- Do the people in your life really expect or need you to do all you feel pressured to do for them?

Affirmation

I set realistic goals. I make powerful decisions about being free and know that things will get done when they get done. I use pressure to create more energy, and at the end of the day I rest and relax even if my to-do list is long. I make decisions according to my Human Design Strategy even if I feel pressure. I breathe and relax knowing there is an abundance of time to get things done.

I am here to be wise about *what's worth doing.*

Conclusion

The configuration of your Energy Centers gives you a powerful peek into how you experience the world. Understanding your Centers can give you deep insights into any patterns and habits that might be keeping you from feeling or acting authentic. Understanding how your Centers function can also give you keys and clues as to how to connect in healthier and more authentic ways in your relationships and teaches you to consciously harness your energy, so that you don't allow your own energy to get hijacked from the energy outside of you.

Your Story

Fill in the following blanks with the information that you've learned from your Human Design chart and this chapter.

My affirmations for Defined and Open Centers:

Head:_____

Ajna: _____

Throat:_____

G-Center: _____

Will: _____

Emotional Solar Plexus: _____

Spleen: _____

Sacral: _____

Root: _____

Chapter 5

PLANETS AND GATES

Your Human Design chart represents the outline of your life story. Your Human Design Type is the role of the main character in your story. Your Profile represents some of your vital character traits. The Centers tell you how you interface with others, what gifts you bring, and what you are designed to receive in your relationships.

The next part of your story, represented by the planets and the Gates in your chart, is going to tell you about the curriculum of your life: what you're here to master, predominant themes you'll encounter as you grow and mature, and how these core traits set up the main challenges that you must master to step into the mature and wise expression of your story.

The Gates represent subtler personality traits that make you who you are. The themes of the Gates are derived from the sixty-four hexagrams from the *I Ching*. Think of them as a modern interpretation of ancient archetypes that have been a spirit of contemplation and study for more than two thousand years.

Each Gate is highlighted by a planet. Each planet also has its own archetypal themes rooted in traditional astrology. As the planets move around the sun, they shine their theme on each of the sixty-four Gates, creating a combination of energies that represent an essential part of your life and soul curriculum.

At the moment of your birth, the planetary positions (the conscious part of your chart) and the Gates they highlighted are locked in place, adding the black Definition (filled-in parts) to your chart.

Three months prior to your birth (or approximately 88 astrological degrees), the red planetary positions (the unconscious part of your chart) and the Gates they highlighted are also locked in place, adding the red Definition (filled-in parts) to your chart.

The black numbers and Gates represent the curriculum for your soul's purpose in this life. The red numbers and Gates represent the curriculum for your life purpose in this lifetime. The combination of both represent your life lessons and challenges and make you who you are in your life story.

Planets

How you experience the energy of each Gate in your chart is influenced by the planet that is highlighting it. On your chart, each planet is demarcated by a symbol that corresponds to its name (see Figure 59).

Understanding the planetary placement of each of the Gates can help illuminate the theme of the Gate that gets expressed. This section will help add detail to the story of who you are and why you're here.

I recommend reading about the planets in conjunction with the Gate descriptions that will follow to gain a clearer picture of how these planetary themes play out for your unique chart. You'll get an idea of how to

---

PLANETARY SYMBOLS

⊙ SUN

⊕ EARTH

☊ NORTH NODE

☋ SOUTH NODE

☽ MOON

☿ MERCURY

♀ VENUS

♂ MARS

♃ JUPITER

♄ SATURN

⚷ CHIRON

♅ URANUS

♆ NEPTUNE

♇ PLUTO

Figure 59: The Planetary Symbols.

weave these pieces of information together through the examples for each of the planetary symbols.

Sun

The Sun represents what you're here to give the world through your life, what you're here to express and transmit. The Sun is a powerful energy, and the Gates in your Sun are typically regarded as the most important—especially the conscious, or black, Sun Gate.

> *Example*: The Sun in Gate 39, also known as the Gate of Provocation

> *Meaning*: You are here to use your provocative nature to help people restore their sense of abundance.

Earth

The Earth's energies are what you need to feel grounded. These energies give you stability. They also support you in strengthening your capacity to express the theme of your Sun energies. Make sure your Earth energies are met so that you can share the gifts of your Sun!

> *Example*: The Earth in Gate 16, known as the Gate of Skills

> *Meaning*: You need to have ample opportunity to experiment and explore what makes you excited in life to be able to fulfill the purpose of the Sun position in your chart.

Moon

The Gates in your Moon are your driver energies; they're why you do what you do.

> *Example*: The Moon in Gate 29, also known as the Gate of Perseverance

Meaning: You're driven by your perseverance and your commitments in life, especially those that you've entered into via your Strategy and Authority. If you are unsure what to commit to or you've committed to the wrong thing, you may find that you lose your motivation and drive.

South Node and North Node

The South Node is the theme you're mastering in the first half of your life, until about age forty, when the planet Uranus is directly opposite the position it was in at the moment of your birth. This is considered by many astrologers to be the midlife in your life story where you mature your life purpose theme.

We move from the South Node theme, which represents your youth, to your North Node theme, your mature self, at this time. When you look at these energies together, they will tell you a lot about the story line of your life: what you're here to learn and master, and then how you live out the mature expression of your chart.

Example: The South Node in Gate 57, also known as the Gate of Intuition; and the North Node in Gate 43, also known as the Gate of Insight

Meaning: You're meant to master your intuitive knowing in the now and release any self-doubt and/or fear of the future. As you mature, you'll use this intuitive knowing to determine the right timing for sharing new, empowered insights.

Mercury

Mercury is all about communication: it outlines what you're here to talk about, what you need to be able to communicate, and how you're here to communicate it. If you are in sales or any communication field, this is an important energy to look at to help you find the consistent theme you're here to explore and share with the world.

Example: Mercury in Gate 8, also known as the Gate of Contribution

Meaning: You're here to communicate with authenticity to bring about change, but only when recognized to do so.

Venus

Venus represents traits, qualities, and characteristics that you value. This planet, along with Mars, is also where you can find the energy you're attracted to in your relationships, romantic and otherwise. So, for example, if you value loyalty and trustworthiness, these themes might be reflected in the Gates highlighted by Venus in your natal chart.

Example: Venus in Gate 32, also known as the Gate of Continuity

Meaning: You value knowing what's valuable in life and are attracted to people who can see the value in you and your ideas and vice versa.

Mars

The Gates in Mars are another area where you'll find lessons you are designed to master in your youth (like the South Node), but these are typically more challenging energies that support you fulfilling your South Node theme. Mars also carries energies for attraction in relationships.

Example: Mars in Gate 38, also known as the Gate of the Fighter

Meaning: Your early life is marked by struggles in mastering what's worth fighting for as you seek purpose and meaning in your life. You're attracted to people who fight for what is meaningful to them.

Jupiter

Jupiter represents the energy of blessings and reward. It tells you about your pathway to your blessings and what you need to share with the world to receive these blessings.

It also works in conjunction with Saturn.

Example: Jupiter in Gate 61, also known as the Gate of Mystery

Meaning: Your blessings arrive as a knowingness that transcends logic, as well as the right timing and people with which to share this often transformative insight.

Saturn

Saturn is your learning energy. The Gates highlighted by Saturn challenge you, meaning that you'll likely experience the shadow or low expression of the Gate in a cataclysmic way that can, ultimately help you learn and mature.

Saturn is also associated with two major life cycles—one at the end of your twenties and one at the end of your fifties. During these phases of your life, your Saturn challenge will be of most importance and at the forefront of your awareness.

The purpose of Saturn is to burn away anything that keeps you from fulfilling your purpose. Your Saturn placement will give you a lot of information about what you need to overcome or learn about to live the full expression of who you are.

As you learn and mature from the placement of Saturn in your chart, you open yourself up to receiving more blessings and benefits, highlighted by the placement of Jupiter in your chart. It's interesting to look at the energy of Saturn and Jupiter both to get a good overview of the payoff for finding the highest expression of your Saturn theme.

Example: Saturn in Gate 28, also known as the Gate of Struggle

Meaning: One of your biggest teachers will arrive in the form of challenges that help you ascertain the meaning of life and discover what is really worth fighting for. When you master this energy, you'll learn to embrace and even find joy in these challenges in life.

Uranus

Uranus shows us where we can be a little strange, different, or unique. Your Uranus placement represents an area of your life where you grow through encountering the unexpected. This energy helps teach you about faith. Because this energy is generational, it also can be where you see shifts in structures, infrastructures, and growth in your generation. It helps you define what your generation is wrestling with in order to evolve and fulfill the full expression of the human story.

> *Example*: Uranus in Gate 36, also known as the Gate of Crisis

> *Meaning*: You are unique in your desires and drive for new, different experiences to help you grow. Your generation is learning to wait for the right timing to act on its desires.

Neptune

The Gates highlighted by Neptune tell you what your spiritual purpose is and what you need to deepen your spiritual connection and stay spiritually connected. This energy can often feel hard to connect with and can seem veiled or intangible.

> *Example*: Neptune in Gate 51, also known as the Gate of Shock

> *Meaning*: You use the shocking or unexpected events of your life or other people's lives to help transform your relationship with Spirit and your spiritual path. Through these catalytic events, you can deepen your connection with your spiritual purpose.

Pluto

Pluto is an energy that grows and expands following the shake-up of the Uranus energies. It often follows a life, death, and rebirth cycle.

Example: Pluto in Gate 46, also known as the Gate of the Love of Body

Meaning: As you grow and change, your experience of being in a body also changes. Your experience of being a soul in a body matures as you go through the cycles of life.

Chiron

Although Chiron is not technically a planet—it's a planetoid discovered in 1978—understanding the Gates of your Chiron can help clarify what you need to master in your personal narrative to deepen your life purpose. Because it's not a planet, it won't show up as colored on your chart, and some chart creation programs don't include it. (If you want a copy of your chart that includes your Chiron placement, go to www.humandesignworkbook.com.)

Chiron's theme will keep repeating itself in your life every time you come to a new level of awareness and expression of yourself. (New level, same devil, so to speak!) It also has a maturing cycle around age fifty (which is especially important for Line 6 Profiles, as mentioned in Chapter 3).

Chiron is a life purpose deepening energy. Once you've done it all, tried it all, and experienced it all, the theme of Chiron comes in to say, "Now what are you going to do with all that?" Anything that stands in the way of you fulfilling your life purpose will come up during your Chiron cycle.

Example: Chiron in Gate 21, also known as the Gate of the Treasurer

Meaning: Your relationship with material things and money will continue to be at the forefront of your growth over time. As you master your need to control things and people, you and your other gifts will become a valuable resource to others.

Next let's explore the Gates. Looking at the Gates and the planets together will help you get a deep sense of your soul curriculum: who you came here to be and what you need to master to create the highest state of well-being in your life.

The Gates

The sixty-four Gates in the Human Design chart correlate to the sixty-four hexagrams from the *I Ching*. I have listed the traditional *I Ching* name with each Gate.

Gates that are colored on your chart represent core life themes that you will encounter throughout your life. These are challenges that you must master to grow into your unique potential, and they can be catalysts for growth and maturation.

To really understand the lesson that your Gates bring you, you will want to look at which planet and planetary theme is highlighting the Gate in your chart. You'll find that information in the numbers on your chart (see Figure 60).

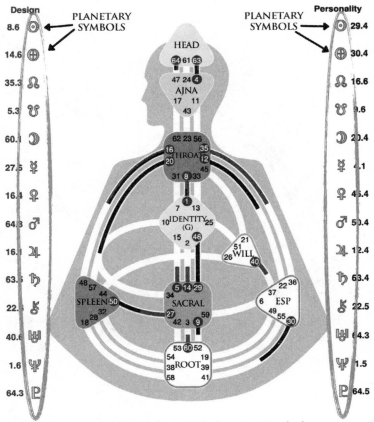

Figure 60: Numbers and planetary symbols
present in the Human Design Chart.

Each planetary symbol has a Gate associated with it. The Gate is the large number next to the planetary symbol.

So, for example, in Figure 61, the Sun is highlighting Gate 29. (You can ignore the smaller decimal number called the "line" of the Gate to the right of the big number. This is covered in my book *Understanding Human Design* if you want to go into more depth.)

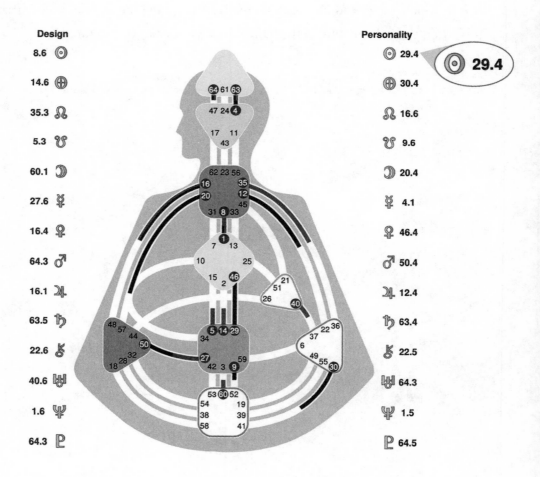

Figure 61: The Sun Highlighting Gate 29.

Each planet highlights a black conscious and a red unconscious Gate. Remember that the black Gates represent your soul purpose and the red Gates represent your life purpose. When interpreting your chart, both Gates bear equal weight and give you deep insights into why you're here and who you're here to be.

You may find, when you look at your chart, that some of the same Gates are highlighted by different planets. In astrology, we call that a "conjunct" planetary position.

You may also find, especially with the slower moving planets like Uranus, Neptune, and Pluto, that the same Gate is highlighted both in the conscious and unconscious Definition. Any time a Gate shows up more than once in your chart, it's a deep theme in your life story that gets played out in many areas and in many ways in your life.

Each Gate listed in this chapter has a description of what the mastery of the Gate theme might look like, the lesson that the Gate brings you, and what the unbalanced expression of the Gate theme might look like. You'll also find a list of contemplations and affirmations to help you think about how this Gate theme might be showing up in your life right now and what it's teaching you.

Remember that the language on different Human Design charts can be slightly different. You can always double-check your chart against the images of the Gates for clarity (beginning with Figure 62).

Gate 1: Self-Expression
I Ching: The Creative

> *Theme*: You have the drive to be relentlessly authentic and to use your life to make a difference in the world. You might be a cultural creative.

> *Life Lessons*: Your contribution to the world is your self-expression. It's not so much what you do as who you are that is the gift. You'll learn to not hide your authentic self.

When Unbalanced: You might hide out, hold back, and not live true to who you really are; or feel stifled or that it's not safe for you to fully express yourself in the world.

Contemplation

- Do you feel safe to fully express who you are in your life? In your work?

- Are you creatively fulfilled? Where in your life do you need to use your creative energy to make change in the world?

- Are you loving yourself enough to allow yourself to be creative?

Affirmation

I am a creative role model. I am here to make a powerful contribution to the world that comes from my heart. When I am relentlessly authentic, my words and energy inspire others to speak their truth and embrace their authentic identity. My life purpose is to show people what being authentic looks like.

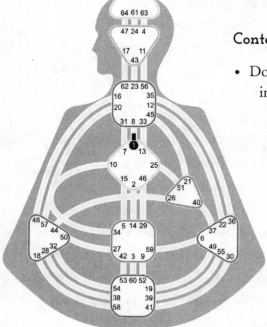

Figure 62: Gate 1.

Gate 2: Keeper of Keys

I Ching: The Receptive

Theme: You value yourself enough to allow yourself to receive all the support and resources you need to fulfill your life purpose.

Life Lessons: Delegate the things that are not yours to do and allow others to help and support you. Trust in the goodness of the Universe and know that you are fully supported. You are worthy of support.

When Unbalanced: You might push help away, and fail to delegate or do everything yourself because you don't believe that you are worthy of support. You might fail to take action that ensures your support because you don't believe you are worthy of success.

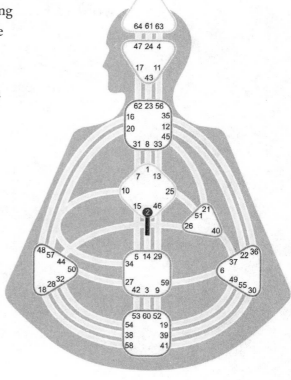

Figure 63: Gate 2.

Contemplation

- How good are you at letting others help and support you?

- Do you value yourself enough to allow yourself to be supported?

- What beliefs need to shift for you to know that you are worthy of support?

Affirmation

I am an irreplaceable and vital part of the world. My life and my purpose are inherently valuable, and I bring to the world something that no one else has ever brought before and will never bring again. To fulfill the story of who I am, I allow myself to receive support.

Gate 3: Ordering

I Ching: Difficulty at the Beginning

> *Theme*: You have the drive to innovate and change and understand that to be truly innovative means to build on what already exists. You will learn to trust that true innovation can only happen when the time is right.

Life Lessons: Be grateful for what you have, pay attention to what is working, and grow from there.

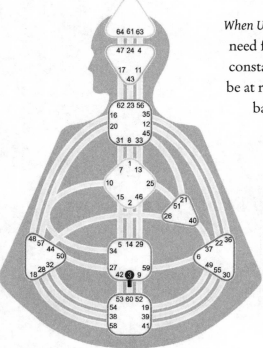

Figure 64: Gate 3.

When Unbalanced: You might be driven by a need for change to such a degree that you are constantly course correcting and at times might be at risk of "throwing the baby out with the bathwater." This constant destruction and rebuild cycle can lead to frustration because you never accomplish the change you seek. You might also push for change without assessing whether others are ready for it.

Contemplation

- When has divine timing worked out in your life? What has waiting taught you?

- Do you trust in divine timing?

- If the opportunity to share your ideas with the world presented itself today, would you be ready? If not, how could you prepare?

Affirmation

I am here to bring change to the world. My natural ability to see what else is possible is my strength and my gift. I patiently cultivate my inspiration and use my understanding of what is needed to help evolve the world.

Gate 4: Answers

I Ching: Youthful Folly

Theme: You understand that the answers you hold are only possibilities. You won't know if they are the right answers unless you experiment and experience them. Stay curious and open-minded to explore whether the answers you hold are correct.

Life Lessons: See the answers you hold as possibilities and give yourself time to imagine, dream, and contemplate. Wait for the right time to translate your answers into action. Be flexible and adaptable with your thinking, and trust yourself and the timing for knowing the right answer.

When Unbalanced: You might defend your answers as truth without knowing whether they work or not, or even make up answers in the face of uncertainty instead of waiting for the answer to reveal itself.

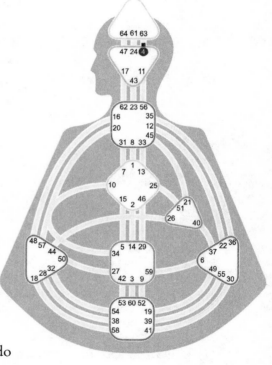

Figure 65: Gate 4.

Contemplation

- What are the next steps you need to take in your creative process?

- What new knowledge and insights do you have as a result of your thoughts, experiences, and meditations?

Affirmation

The culmination of my thoughts and experiences grants me knowledge about how I can proceed confidently and faithfully in the future.

Gate 5: Patterns

I Ching: Waiting

Theme: You'll cultivate and protect daily practices and habits as a way of creating stability and consistency in your life and understand that you do better when you have consistent habits. This can be as simple as having a cup of coffee at the same time every day or as complex as committing to a spiritual practice. To make change, you need time to create a new rhythm or habits.

Life Lessons: Cultivate a daily practice that grounds you in consistency and supports you in your growth and mastery.

When Unbalanced: You might be so stuck in your habits that you struggle to adapt, pivot, or make a change.

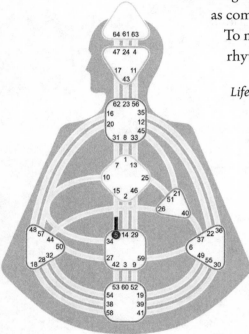

Figure 66: Gate 5.

Contemplation

- Are your patterns and habits supporting your health and momentum? Do you need to change any habits that might be keeping you stuck in a pattern that isn't productive?

- Do you need to create new habits that are healthier and more supportive?

Affirmation

I create best when I have a foundation of consistency and a practice that supports my mastery. I am fluid and adaptable when I keep my daily practice of self-renewal and self-care. My consistency and patterns help ground others and make me reliable and dependable.

Gate 6: Friction

I Ching: Conflict

Theme: You have the ability to know when, how, and what work needs to be done to create impact and sustainable resources for others.

Life Lessons: Trust in right timing, and know that when it's time for you to share who you are and what you have, the conditions will be right for you to be seen and heard by the people who will be impacted by you.

When Unbalanced: You might have such a strong sense of scarcity that you feel the need to fight for or take what you think you don't have. You might fight to be seen and heard and consequently push people away or organize people around the idea that something is missing from their lives, inspiring an energy of competition and fighting.

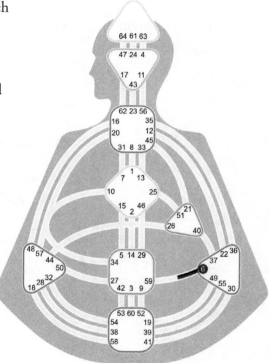

Figure 67: Gate 6.

Contemplation

- Do you trust in your support and abundance? If not, what needs to change?

- Do you believe in enough? What is happening in your life right now that is proof of your support?

- Are you nurturing yourself so that you stay sustainable and have more to give?

- Are you ready to be seen and heard? How comfortable are you with your visibility? What needs to be healed, released, aligned, or brought to your awareness for you to be fully seen and heard?

Affirmation

I surrender myself to life. I surrender myself to my destiny and all that it means to be me. I trust that the timing will be right for me to share who I am and what I have in a meaningful and abundant way. I know that I am always supported, and I relax and trust in my support.

Gate 7: Self in Interaction

I Ching: The Army

Theme: You know that supporting people in a leadership role is powerful. Like the chief of staff, the person who coordinates and creates behind the scenes is often more powerful than the figurehead.

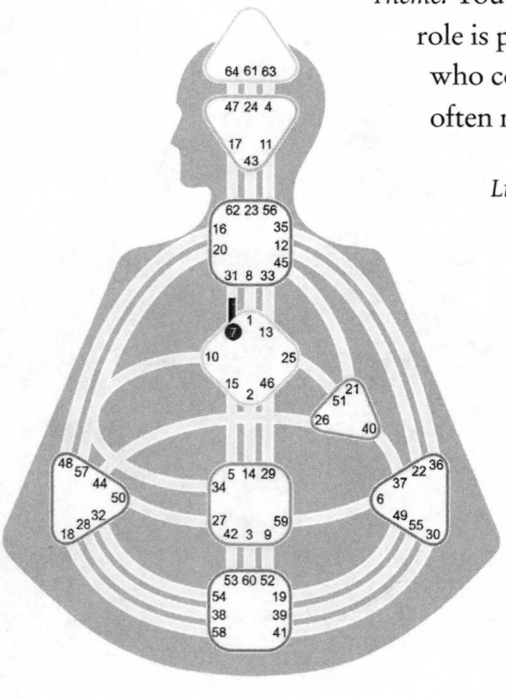

Life Lessons: Let go of the need to be in the spotlight and instead serve leadership in a supportive capacity. Master the art of influence through supporting those who appear to be in charge.

When Unbalanced: You might feel unseen and unrecognized or want to be the figurehead and forgo your natural place as the support person.

Figure 68: Gate 7.

Contemplation

- Where do you need to take action in your life? What do you need to do to lead yourself toward fulfilling your dream?

- What kind of influence and recognition would you like to be experiencing? What has kept you from recognition in the past? Is there anything you need to change to increase your light?

Affirmation

I take leadership over my life and know that I will be called to share my influence with the world. I am empowered and trust the Universe to take me exactly where I need to go to impress my authentic expression on the face of the world.

Gate 8: Contribution
I Ching: Holding Together

Theme: You push the edges and boundaries of authentic self-expression and realize that being the full expression of your authentic self is your life purpose. You use your authentic expression to inspire others.

Life Lessons: Value yourself and who you are and have the courage to be relentlessly authentic no matter what anyone else says or does.

When Unbalanced: You might hold back and hide your truth or compromise who you are for the sake of fitting in or safety. You might bend to the pressure of creating something meaningful and try to figure out that contribution with your mind instead of your heart.

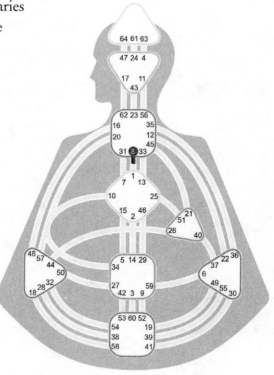

Figure 69: Gate 8.

Contemplation

- If you could live an uncompromising life, what would it look like?

- Do you dream of making a contribution to the world? What is it? What do you need to do to bring it forth? Is there anything stopping you?

Affirmation

My contribution to humanity is important. I commit to expressing my authenticity to its fullest extent. The world needs me to play the role I intend to play, and the greatest contribution I make is to share my light, my love, my self with the world. I never hold back. I radiate. I am a crucial part of the light of the wholeness of humankind.

Gate 9: Focus

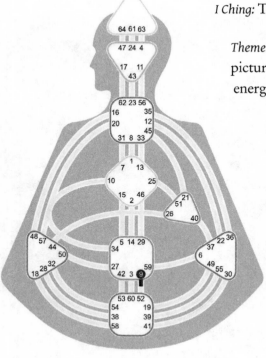

Figure 70: Gate 9.

I Ching: The Taming Power of the Small

Theme: You have the ability to see the big picture and prioritize where to focus your energy.

Life Lessons: Cultivate a lifestyle and a way of creating that supports you staying focused on your goals and intentions. See beyond distraction.

When Unbalanced: You might feel pressured to figure out where to place your focus or overwhelmed and confused by too many options. You might not be able to see the relationship between ideas and actions and miss important details.

Contemplation

- What do you need to do to make your dreams come true? (These are practical things, like writing a book, test-driving a car, building a website, taking a class.)

- What do you need the Universe to do? (These are things that may feel beyond your control, such as attracting the perfect clients, friends, or lover or providing the perfect information and support.)

Affirmation

I trust the Universe to provide me with everything I need to make my dreams come true. While I wait for the perfect unfoldment of my dreams, I take powerful steps and implement important details to prepare for the manifestation of my intentions. I relax knowing that I am doing my part in cocreating my life.

Gate 10: Love of Self

I Ching: Treading

> *Theme:* You see your love for yourself as the spirit of your true creative power, and you nurture yourself, set good boundaries, and embrace an empowered mindset that disallows a victim consciousness.

> *Life Lessons:* Love yourself and take responsibility for your own creations.

> *When Unbalanced:* You might question your lovability or struggle to prove your love-worthiness; you might give up and settle for less than what you deserve or blame others for your circumstances and situations.

Contemplation

- What old energies and victim stories do you need to release?

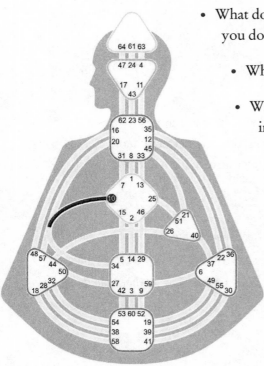

- What does power mean to you? What could you do to feel more empowered?

- What do you love about yourself?

- What actions could you take that are in alignment with your self-love?

Figure 71: Gate 10.

Affirmation

I honor the miracle that I am. I am a unique, divine creation, and I know there is no one like me in this world. I make choices and take actions that are honoring of my divine magnificence, and I surround myself with people who support, nurture, and inspire me. I am powerful and in charge of my life direction. I make choices that allow me to fulfill my divine potential, and being the fullest expression of myself, I create the space for others to do the same.

Gate 11: Ideas

I Ching: Peace

Theme: You are a vessel for ideas, and you understand that those ideas are for you to hold and protect until the right person comes along for you to share them with. You know that not all ideas are yours to build upon, and you use the power of your inspiration to stimulate the imagination of yourself and others.

Life Lessons: Hold on to ideas until the time is right to either share or implement them. Not all your ideas should be implemented. Use the power of your creative thinking to inspire others.

When Unbalanced: You might feel pressured and anxious to act on all your ideas, resulting in a series of scattered and frenetic efforts that leave you feeling unfulfilled and frustrated.

Contemplation

- What are some of your achievements and accomplishments of the last few weeks? How could you improve upon what you've done? What did you learn?

- What ideas have you had this week?

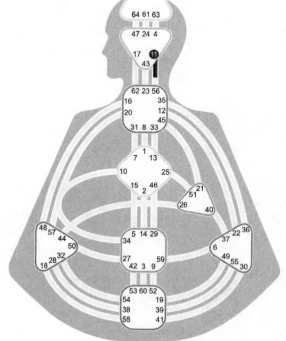

Figure 72: Gate 11.

Affirmation

I honor my inner creative process. I am grateful for every lesson and adventure I have, and I know that each story adds beautiful, rich threads to the tapestry of my life and the story of humanity. I relax and enjoy the quest for truth, knowing that the more I learn, the more I grow, and the learning and growing never stop. I allow myself to savor every moment and serve as the creative vessel that I am. I relax, breathe, trust, and let the ideas flow.

Gate 12: Caution

I Ching: Standstill

> *Theme*: Your voice is an expression of transformation and a vehicle for divine insight. The words you speak, the insights and creativity you

share, have the power to change others and the world. This energy is so powerful that people must be ready to receive it. When you are articulate, then the timing is correct. If you struggle to find the words, have the courage to wait until things feel more aligned.

Life Lessons: Try not to push your ideas out into the world with people who are not ready for what you have to share. Learn to trust that your words are important and wait for readiness to protect the integrity of your ideas.

When Unbalanced: You might struggle to articulate what you know and push against right timing and the receptiveness of others to your insights and ideas.

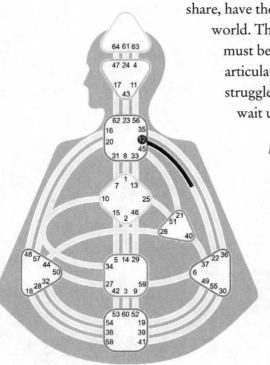

Figure 73: Gate 12.

Contemplation

- Are you using willpower or divine power to create?

- Do you feel stuck? If so, what do you need to do to keep moving forward?

- Is it time to share your thoughts, ideas, and divine inspirations with others?

- What playful things can you do to inspire your creative energy?

Affirmation

In my expression of my intention, I stay open to the voice and words of the Divine. My words, expression, and creation are divinely guided, and I speak the perfect words to transmit the beauty of who I am and what I create. My voice is heard and valued, and I continue to share my insights and my experiences as part of my creative process. My divine perspective supports me in evolving my ideas and creations.

Gate 13: The Listener

I Ching: The Fellowship of Man

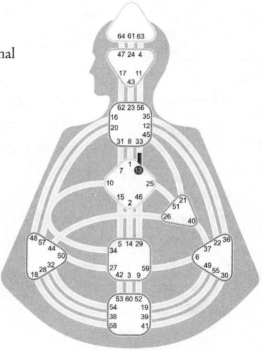

Theme: You use the strength of personal narrative to create with power and intention.

Life Lessons: Remember that the story you tell about your life and who you are sets the tone and the direction for your experiences in the world. When you hold a personal narrative that embraces your strengths and the fulfillment of your potential, your life begins to reflect this as truth.

Figure 74: Gate 13.

When Unbalanced: You might get stuck in old stories, hurts, and resentments that create a personal narrative of victimhood and blame that keeps you from moving forward in your life with ease and healthy momentum.

Contemplation

- What is the status of your ego? Are you comfortable serving the higher good without recognition? Are there areas where you are still motivated by a need to prove something?

- What can you do to listen and truly hear others better? What do you need to do to hear and listen to your own guidance better?

- Are you taking time for yourself to allow for clarity? Do you see the truth of your past? What pieces from the past do you still need to release?

Affirmation

I am a servant to the Divine. In my quiet retreat, I align with my higher purpose, and I take actions that are of service to the greater good.

Each day I ask that my mind, eyes, words, heart, hands, body, light, and being be used in divine service. I am grateful for all that has come before me, and I ask that I take the lessons from my past and use them to be of service to others. I listen carefully to the words and true meanings of others. I allow myself to see the truth behind all words so that I always know the divine meaning of each communication.

I am clear. I am present. I take my time to respond meaningfully. I speak words that open doors of opportunities to others. I hold a sacred space for humanity to come together to fulfill its highest purpose. I lead with love.

Gate 14: Power Skills

I Ching: Possession in Great Measure

Theme: You are at peace about having resources and trust that everything you need will show up in alignment with your spiritual purpose. The resources you have allow you to increase resources available to others. You will change the definition of work, no longer working for material gain, but for the sake of transforming the world and being in the flow of life. You know that support flows from alignment with your heart.

Life Lessons: Make peace with money. Trust that you will always have opportunities, and trust in sufficiency.

When Unbalanced: You might panic about work and money, and overwork or accept work that you don't want simply for the sake of material gain.

Contemplation

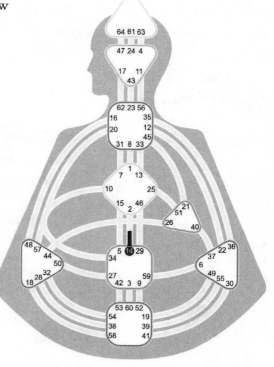

Figure 75: Gate 14.

- What are you doing right now that you find inspiring and delicious? Can you make a commitment to yourself to follow at least one of these inspirations each day?

- What would your life look like if you only followed your passion? What would you be doing? What would your life feel like? What would your energy level be?

- Do you trust the Universe to support you in following your bliss? Is it okay to make money doing what you love? Can you do what you love and know that you will be supported?

Affirmation

I respond to the things that bring me joy. I pay attention to my excitement and passion and allow myself to trust that the Universe is deliciously conspiring to find ways to support me in the pursuit of my passion. I do what I want to do. I do what feels correct. I honor my joy and excitement and commit to feeling good, knowing that this is the most important contribution I can make to the planet at this time.

Gate 15: Extremes

I Ching: Modesty

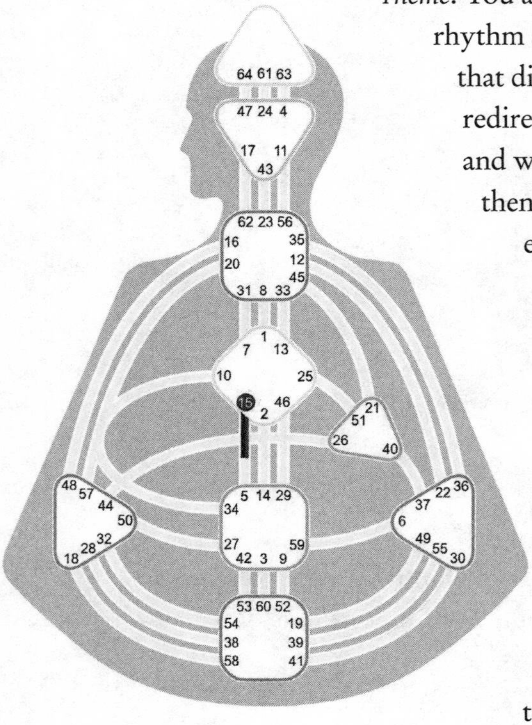

Figure 76: Gate 15.

Theme: You are able to trust your own flow and rhythm and understand that you will have cycles that disrupt old patterns and force you to redirect. You set parameters for your creativity and work within them when it feels right and then rest in between. Nature has rhythm and extremes. You are here to change the old rhythms and patterns to align with greater compassion.

Life Lessons: Follow your own flow and rhythm and honor your boom-and-bust cycles of energy and creativity.

When Unbalanced: You might judge yourself for failing to have habits and consistency. You might struggle to find the right habits when you're not here to be habituated; you are here to follow the flow.

Contemplation

- What contributions are you making to humanity? Are you acknowledging your service? Do you need or want to deepen your commitment?

- What role does rhythm play in your life? Does your personal rhythm bring you joy? Enhance your creations? Fulfill your intentions? Do you need to experiment or change your rhythm?

Affirmation

My life adds to the greatness of humanity. My work benefits the world. I accept unconditionally the broad spectrum of diversity and rhythm that makes up humanity, and I surrender to the larger flow of life. I am awed by the magnificence of humankind, and my awe inspires me to be of service to the greater good.

Gate 16: Skills

I Ching: Enthusiasm

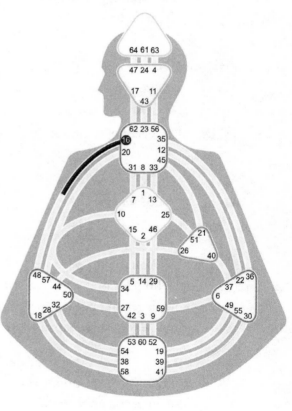

Theme: You have the courage to leap into action and inspire others to act, even if you don't know all the details or exactly how your journey will unfold. You trust that the timing is right, and have faith in the outcome.

Life Lessons: Prepare when it's necessary. Assess whether you are genuinely ready before your enthusiasm overrides your need to build a solid foundation first.

When Unbalanced: You might fail to do your homework before you act, sometimes causing you to

Figure 77: Gate 16.

scramble or face chaotic results. You might quit before trying because the fear of making a mistake is too strong.

Contemplation

- What dreams are beginning to come to fruition? What is your experimentation teaching you? What are you needing to tweak?

- What beliefs may be part of creating the manifestation of your experiments? Are there any old beliefs that you need to release?

- Can you imagine the full, enthusiastic expression of your unique gifts and talents?

Affirmation

I am a faith-filled, contagious force. I take guided actions and trust my intuition and awareness to let me know when I am prepared and ready to leap into expanding my experience and mastery. My enthusiasm inspires others to trust in themselves and take their own giant leaps of growth.

Gate 17: Opinions

I Ching: Following

Theme: You use the power of your mind to imagine what else is possible in the human condition. You use your thoughts to inspire others to think bigger and bolder, and your words to inspire and set the stage for creating energy that expands potential.

Life Lessons: Accept that your mind generates powerful possibilities and trust that when the timing is right you'll find the right people to share these powerful ideas with.

When Unbalanced: You might push your ideas and opinions without waiting for people to be ready and accept your opinions as fact without researching whether what you believe is actually true.

Contemplation

- What do you do with ideas and inspirations that spark your enthusiasm? Are you good at holding on to ideas and allowing the right people to be drawn to the germinating phase of your creation?

- What does the phrase "to serve" mean to you? Are you being of service? Do you need to do more? Are you serving yourself as the foundation? Can you serve yourself without guilt?

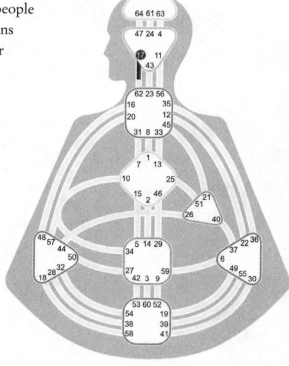

Figure 78: Gate 17.

Affirmation

I wait to offer my insights until I am asked. I am aware that what is true for me is not always true for others. Each one of us has our own unique journey, and our perceptions create our understandings. I wait for the right people to ask me for my understandings. I know that when people ask, they will truly value my insights. My insights are valuable to those who seek them. In order to be valued, I must first be of service. I serve the truth and wait for those who are aligned with my truth.

Gate 18: Correction

I Ching: Work on What Has Been Spoilt

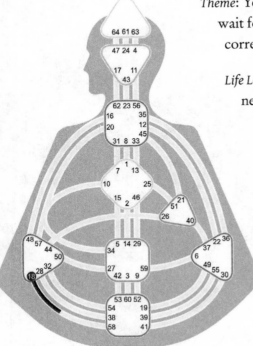

Figure 79: Gate 18.

Theme: You see a pattern that needs correcting and wait for the right timing and circumstances to correct and align it.

Life Lessons: Trust your intuitive sense of what needs to be corrected. Wait for the readiness of others before you share.

When Unbalanced: You might be hypercritical and self-righteous about what you think others need to do to fix their performance.

Contemplation

- What do you need to work on releasing? Judging? Forgiving?

- When you look at your life, what patterns of success and/or self-sabotage are you aware of? What patterns keep repeating? What can you do to shift these patterns?

- In your creative process, what needs to be tweaked to be brought into a more aligned expression?

Affirmation

My entire life is a process of ever-expanding perfection. Where I am right now is the sum of all my experiences. As I learn and grow, so does my understanding and consciousness. I am perfect right now. My so-called mistakes are catalysts for my growth, and I enjoy correcting patterns and bringing more and more alignment with my divinity into my life! Each and every day offers opportunities to grow and expand and I am grateful!

Gate 19: Wanting

I Ching: Approach

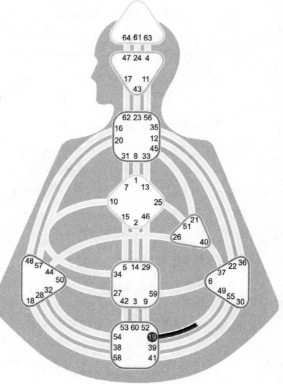

Theme: You are able to sense the emotional needs of others and your community and know how to bring the emotional energy back into alignment sustainably. You are emotionally vulnerable and present to increase heart-to-heart connections.

Life Lessons: Don't let your sensitivity to others cause you to give up your own needs and wants or to retreat from the world. Be compassionate but not codependent. Learn how to craft true intimacy and emotional connection.

When Unbalanced: You might be so emotionally dialed in to others that you give up what you want or fail to ask for what you need. You might hide out from overwhelming emotions because you're too sensitive or fail to deal with truth or conflict because it feels too emotionally challenging.

Figure 80: Gate 19.

Contemplation

- What cycles in your life are coming to an end? Are you resisting or allowing these conclusions? Is there anything you need to do to create space for the beginning of a new cycle?

- What lessons have you learned from this cycle? Which blessings are you taking with you into the new cycle? Where do you have new clarity?

- What does intimacy mean to you? Are your needs being met? Are you meeting the needs of your partner? Are you asking clearly for what you want? Are you allowing your partner to give to you? Are there places where you need to master fulfilling your own intimacy needs?

Affirmation

I am deeply aware of the emotional needs and energy of others. My sensitivity and awareness give me insights that allow me to create intimacy and vulnerability in my relationships. I am aware and attuned to the emotional frequency around me, and I help support a high frequency of emotional alignment. I honor my own emotional needs as the foundation of what I share with others.

Gate 20: Metamorphosis
I Ching: Contemplation

Theme: You trust your intuition and know what needs to be set in place, what people need to be gathered, what skills need to be mastered, and when the time is right. You trust in the right timing and heed the intuition to prepare.

Life Lessons: Be patient and trust in right timing; power is amplified when the timing is aligned.

When Unbalanced: You might jump into action before it's time and fail to reap the full potential of what you've envisioned. You might leap from thing to thing because your impatience keeps you from waiting for the right timing.

Contemplation

- How do you feel about "not doing"?

- Are there places in your life where you are busy without direction? Are you battling burnout? Are you being as effective as you'd like to be?

- Are there places in your life where you need to take leadership? How about delegate?

- How do you define your personal power? Are you fully activating it?

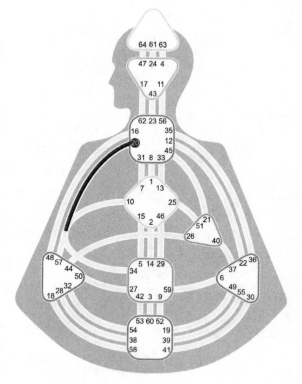

Figure 81: Gate 20.

Affirmation

Just because I can do it doesn't mean that I have to or that I should. I use my Strategy to determine my actions, and I only do the things that are correct for me. I am a door to cosmic perfection and the entrance point for actions that create the divine order. It is in my not-doing that my doing becomes evident.

Gate 21: The Treasurer

I Ching: Biting Through

> *Theme*: You regulate your inner and outer environment to sustain a vibrational frequency that reflects your true value. You are self-generous and set boundaries that maintain your value and support you in being

sustainable in the world. You take the necessary actions to honor your unique role in the cosmic plan.

Life Lessons: Let go of the need to control others; master controlling yourself.

When Unbalanced: You might overcompensate for a feeling of being out of control by trying to control circumstances, situations, or other people.

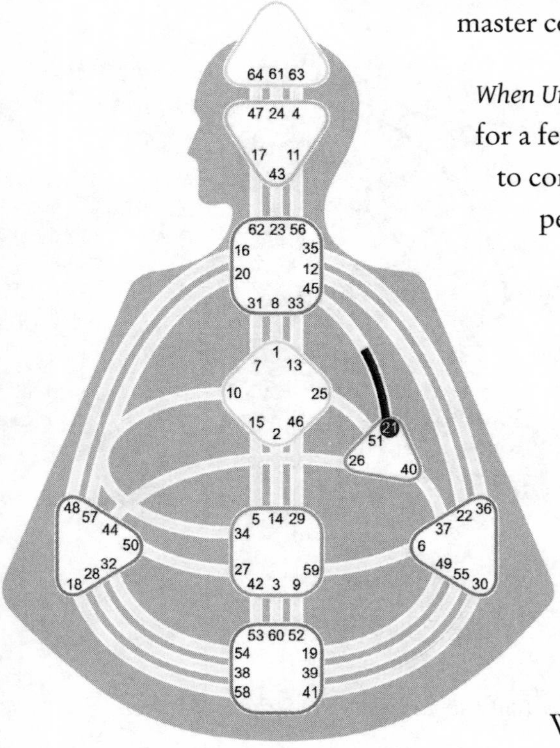

Figure 82: Gate 21.

Contemplation

- Where in your life do you need to let go?

- What do you need to do to allow others to express themselves and to hold a space for their freedom?

- How might you deepen your spiritual practice and connection? What old beliefs and fears need to be released so that you can move more deeply into trust?

Affirmation

I control my thoughts and my actions. I release my need to control others. I trust that the Universe will provide all the serendipitous encounters and the magic necessary to create the manifestation of my desires. I use my energy to manage myself. I trust that my mindset and my intentional actions will encourage the Universe to conspire with me. I lead by example.

Gate 22: Openness

I Ching: Grace

Theme: You know that you are fully supported by the universal flow of abundance. You pursue your passion and your unique contribution to the world no matter what, trusting that you will be given what you need when you need it.

Life Lessons: Have the courage to follow your passion and know that you'll be supported. Surrender and trust in your support.

When Unbalanced: You might hold yourself back from following your truth and your passion because you're afraid that it won't be supported or it will be meaningless. You might use drama as a way of distracting yourself or avoiding your alignment with your creative passion.

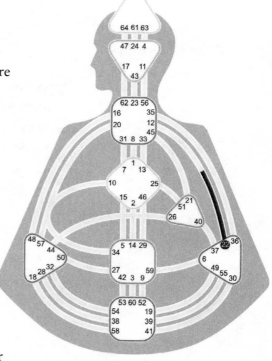

Figure 83: Gate 22.

Contemplation

- When faced with the emotional energy and drama of others, what is your Strategy to allow and be aware? What are your methods for detaching?

- Do you trust that your passions and the fulfillment of your creative desires are supported? What old ideas do you need to surrender to

allow yourself to follow your passion and trust the direction that it
will lead you?

Affirmation

*In the face of divine order, I stand with grace and presence. I see and integrate, evaluate, and
share my awareness. I articulate the conclusions with grace and correct timing. I use my ability
to perceive correct awareness to bring my awareness and understandings to others. I am the
calm within the storm. I follow my passion with the awareness that I am fully supported and
that my alignment with my creative expression is the gift I am here to share with the world.*

Gate 23: Assimilation
I Ching: Splitting Apart

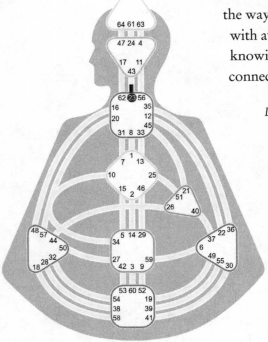

Theme: You are able to offer insights that transform
the way others think. You share what you know
with awareness of right timing. You trust your
knowingness as an expression of your spiritual
connection.

Life Lessons: Wait for the right timing and
the right people before you share your
transformative insights and ideas.

When Unbalanced: You might push
your innovative ideas out into
the world before people are
ready to receive them and then
misinterpret the bad timing as a
perception that the idea itself is bad.

Figure 84: Gate 23.

THE HUMAN DESIGN WORKBOOK

Contemplation

- What do you do to hold your vision? What part of your daily practice supports you in holding the energy of your intention?

- How does it feel when you don't know how something will manifest? How long do you hold your intention? Do you have the patience to wait for the right thing? Can you let go of your backup plan and trust the divine order? Are you preparing with small acts of faith that will show the Universe that you are ready for the next step in your assignment?

- Do you have the courage to hold on to a vision, even when no one else understands it at the moment? Is it okay for you to be on your own with your intention? How do you feel about not fitting in? When do you quit? When do you hold steady?

Affirmation

My greatest strength is my ability to be still and wait to be asked to share the vision I hold. I stand with great confidence in my knowingness, and I trust that I know and hold the intention to create dynamic change for my own good and for the greater good of the whole.

Gate 24: Rationalization

I Ching: Returning

Theme: You recognize that all experiences have the potential for growth and expansion and redefine your stories to reflect what you learned and how you grew. You are grateful for all your life experiences to liberate yourself from stories that no longer serve you.

Life Lessons: Find the blessings in all situations—even the painful ones. Use painful circumstances as a way to grow in your own power and sense of value. Don't settle for less than you deserve.

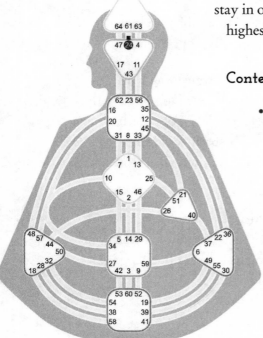

Figure 85: Gate 24.

When Unbalanced: You might rationalize victimhood or stay in old, stuck patterns that don't support the highest expression of your value.

Contemplation

- What are all the things that feel good and are working in your life?

  - What have your greatest challenges taught you?

  - Where might you be settling for less than what you want or deserve?

Affirmation

I give my attention to my progress and all that is good. I focus on what is working, what is aligning, and I trust that all that is good will grow. I celebrate my successes and focus on creating more success by simply attending to that which is correct for me.

Gate 25: Love of Spirit

I Ching: Innocence

Theme: You trust the divine order and connect with God/Spirit as the path to creating well-being in your life. You remember that your life serves an irreplaceable role in the cosmic plan and honor that role and live from it.

Life Lessons: See your life as part of a higher purpose. Take the right action even if you don't know how it's going to turn out.

When Unbalanced: You might act with hatred and self-interest. You might forget the true purpose of your life and act recklessly.

Contemplation

- How much do you trust in divine order?

- How connected do you feel to your higher purpose? Do you trust God/Spirit/the Universe? Enough to take bold action?

Affirmation

I am perfectly prepared to take my place in the divine order. I know that my intentions can and will be fulfilled according to divine mind, and I relax and trust. I know that there are greater unexpected outcomes that are for my higher good and trust that all is well. I turn a blind eye to how things look and know that the truth will be revealed to me when I need to know. The Spirit of God within me is the spirit of all my good.

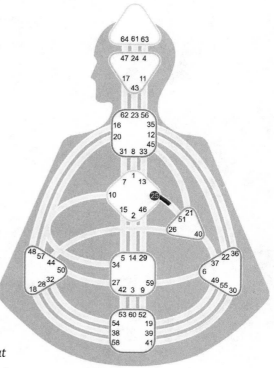

Figure 86: Gate 25.

Gate 26: The Trickster

I Ching: The Taming Power of the Great

> *Theme*: You live in moral, energetic, identity, physical, and resource integrity with courage and trust. You set clear boundaries and take the actions necessary to preserve the integrity of your right place.

Life Lessons: Strengthen your self-worth so that you can live sustainably and in integrity with yourself and others.

When Unbalanced: You might overcompensate for low self-worth by being out of integrity with yourself, with your choices, and with others.

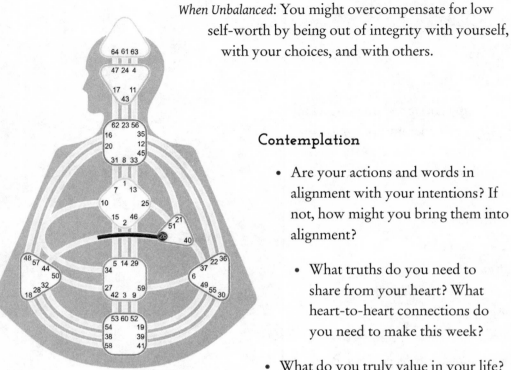

Figure 87: Gate 26.

Contemplation

- Are your actions and words in alignment with your intentions? If not, how might you bring them into alignment?

  - What truths do you need to share from your heart? What heart-to-heart connections do you need to make this week?

- What do you truly value in your life? Are you sharing your appreciation?

Affirmation

I speak and act with integrity. My actions and words are in alignment with my intentions. I take my time to speak the perfect words because I know that my words are representations of my heart and my inspirations. I care deeply about my impact, and I listen with love to those around me. I take my time and act in alignment with my values, and I share my heart freely with my loved ones.

Gate 27: Responsibility

I Ching: Nourishment

Theme: You support, nurture, and lift others up. You sense and act on what is necessary to increase the well-being of others and the world. You feed people with healthy food and nourishment to ensure that they thrive. You hold others accountable for their own self-love and self-empowerment.

Life Lessons: Care without overcaring. Allow others to assume responsibility for their own challenges and choices. Accept other people's values. Don't let guilt cause you to compromise what is good and right for you.

When Unbalanced: You might be codependent, feel guilty, or find yourself overgiving or overcaring.

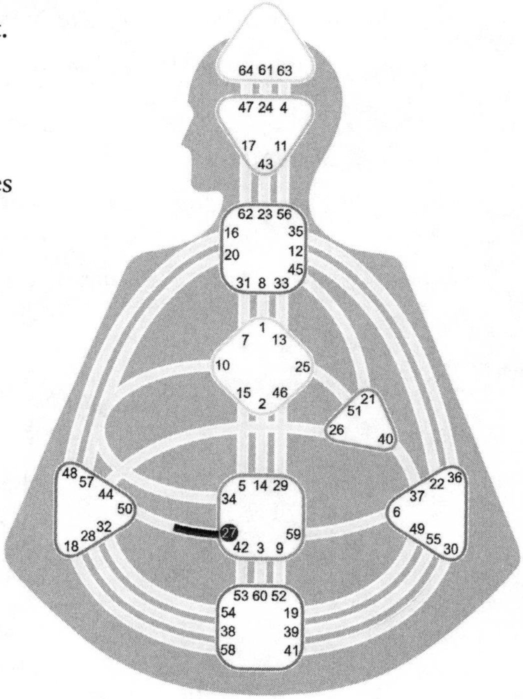

Figure 88: Gate 27.

Contemplation

- What are you taking responsibility for that you need to release? Is guilt helping you hold on to something that you need to let go of? Can you release the guilt?

- What small acts of compassion are you not doing because you don't think it will do any good? Can you give yourself permission to do them anyway?

- With the awareness that you are responsible for your own reality, is there anything about how you are creating your reality that you'd like to change? Do you need to take better care of yourself?

Affirmation

I am responsible for aligning with what is. I trust that when faced with challenges, I will also know exactly what to do. I take care of myself and then others so that my energy is strong and my capacity to care is limitless and empowering.

Gate 28: Struggle

I Ching: The Preparedness of the Great

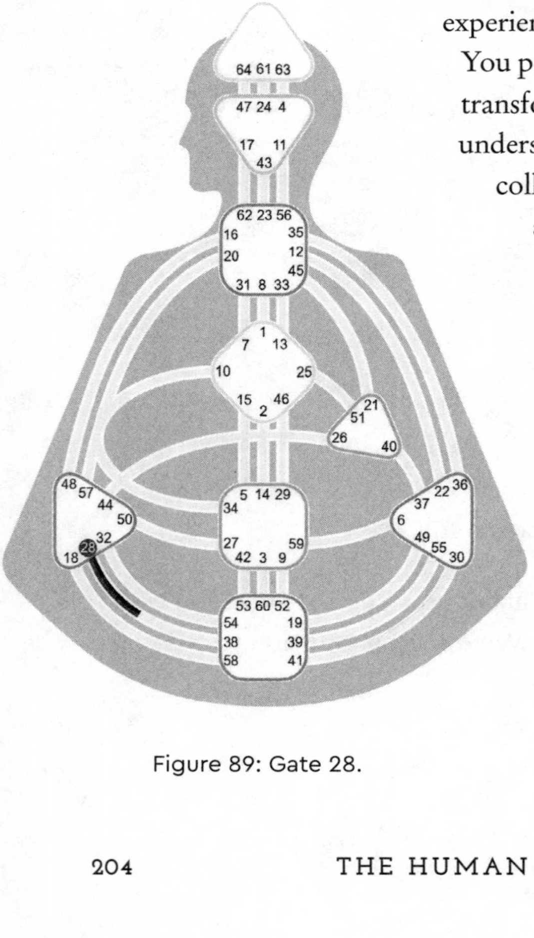

Theme: You learn to share from your personal experience—your struggles and your triumphs. You persevere, knowing that your adventures transform life into a meaningful journey, and understand that your struggles help deepen the collective ideas about what is truly valuable and worthy of creating.

Life Lessons: Work toward what's truly valuable and worthy of your effort and commitment.

When Unbalanced: You might fight, struggle, and press against everything without regard to whether the end result is worth the fight.

Contemplation

- What in your life is worth living for?

Figure 89: Gate 28.

- How have your past struggles shaped who you are today?

Affirmation

I am fully alive, and I am constantly present to the energy and possibility of life. I commit myself and my energy to pursuing the dreams that are vital, inspiring, and truly worthy of my efforts and endurance.

Gate 29: Perseverance

I Ching: The Abysmal

Theme: You respond to committing to the right thing. Your perseverance and determination change the narrative of the world and show people what is possible. Your devotion sets the tone for the direction that life takes you.

Life Lessons: Commit to the right things. Persevere and stay focused on putting your efforts toward what feels good, right, and aligned.

When Unbalanced: You might overcommit and burn out or fail to commit to what brings you the deepest joy.

Contemplation

- What are you committed to? What actions do you need to take to reflect and deepen that commitment?

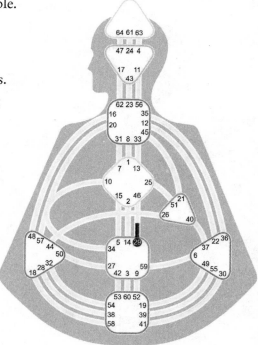

Figure 90: Gate 29.

- What do you need to learn to say no to? What do you want to say yes to?

Affirmation

I carefully examine my actions and make sure that my commitments are in alignment with my intentions. I only say yes to the things I know will bring me closer to fulfilling my dreams, and I enter into my commitments according to my Human Design Strategy.

Gate 30: Desire
I Ching: Clinging Fire

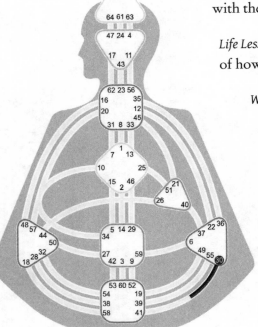

Figure 91: Gate 30.

Theme: You can sustain a dream, intention, or vision until you bring it into form. You inspire passion in others with the power of your dream.

Life Lessons: Sustain your intensity and be aware of how your intensity impacts others.

When Unbalanced: You might burn out if your passion isn't focused on what you truly want, is not in alignment, or is suppressed. You might allow the intensity of your passion to burn others out.

Contemplation

- What do you want in life? What do you choose to experience in your finances, your health, your relationships, your creative fulfillment, your spiritual life, and your lifestyle?

- What distractions do you need to remove to keep your focus sharp?

- What are you passionate about? Are you free to express your passion? What keeps you from your passion?

Affirmation

I am clear about my intentions and desires. I honor myself for creating the space to bring forth my dreams and intentions. My life is completely open to receive, and I stand in a passionate place of anticipation for the manifestation of my desires. I only focus on what I want. My vision is true, and my passion is fed by the fire of my heart. I am unwavering and powerfully focused.

Gate 31: Democracy

I Ching: Influence

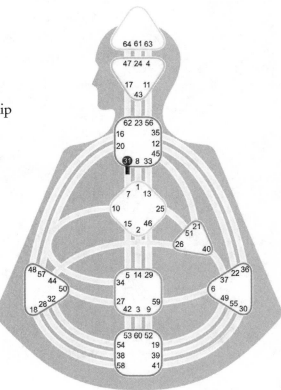

Theme: You are able to listen, learn, and serve the people you lead. You assume and value your right leadership position as the voice for the people.

Life Lessons: Lead as a representative for the greater good. Lead from the heart, not the ego.

When Unbalanced: You might seize leadership positions for personal gain or fail to lead when it's necessary out of fear of vulnerability.

Contemplation

- How do you feel about your leadership ability?

Figure 92: Gate 31.

- What experiences from your past would help you figure out what kind of leader you'd like to be?

Affirmation

I assume my position of natural leadership when I am asked or invited to assume influence. My words, my thoughts, my ideas, and my dream are important and worthy of sharing with the right people.

Gate 32: Continuity

I Ching: Duration

Theme: You know what needs to be done to make a dream a reality: setting the stage, being ready, trusting that the timing will unfold as needed to serve the highest good of all. You translate divine inspiration into readiness.

Life Lessons: Trust the process. Allow for divine timing and take care of the details while you wait for the timing to align. Be patient.

When Unbalanced: You might feel frustrated and scared that you're not doing enough or that you're going to miss an opportunity if you don't act. You might push too hard against right timing and put all your effort into trying to control an outcome.

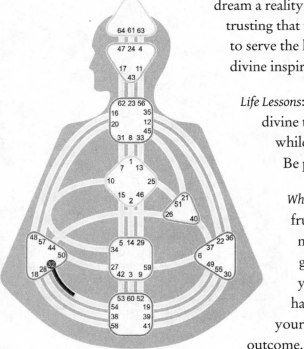

Figure 93: Gate 32.

Contemplation

- What would an unlimited life look like? What would you do? What would your business look like?

- What new leaps of faith do you need to take? What new commitments do you need to make?

Affirmation

My dreams always come true. I would not be given an inspiration without also being given the capacity to realize it into form. I have everything I need to fulfill my dream. I trust the process. I trust in right timing.

Gate 33: Privacy

I Ching: Retreat

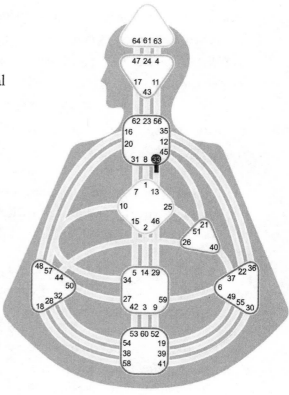

Theme: You can translate a personal experience into an empowering narrative that teaches and gives direction to others, finding power from the pain. You wait for the right time to transform or share a narrative so that it has the greatest impact on the heart of another.

Life Lessons: Translate the pain and hurt of the past into an empowered story of survival. Forgive and move forward; do not stay rooted in the pain of the past.

Figure 94: Gate 33.

When Unbalanced: You might be stuck in old stories, unable to move forward because you can't forgive the events of the past.

Contemplation

- If you have not seen the results in forward momentum in your life that you intend, what do you think is holding you back? What story line are you living?

- If you could rewrite your story, what would change? What would the end result be?

Affirmation

I continue my journey inward, working with the cycles of creation and repose. My focus now is on myself, my journey, my past, and the evolution of my future. I relax and trust that what is hidden will be revealed, the truth will be demonstrated, and my greatest power is in divine timing. I trust. I wait. I know. I grow.

Gate 34: Power

I Ching: The Power of the Great

Theme: You respond to opportunities to unify the right people around a transformative and powerful idea when the timing and circumstances are correct.

Life Lessons: Trust in right timing. Don't jump the gun on an idea — wait and see what shows up so that you're not wasting effort pushing something that isn't ready yet.

When Unbalanced: You might feel exhausted, powerless, and frustrated from trying to make your ideas happen when the timing isn't right. You might fail to take stock of your readiness or the readiness of others before launching a new project and feeling perpetually frustrated because it never turns out the way you'd hoped.

Contemplation

- How are you leveraging your power and energy? What do you need to stop doing to create space for what you truly want?

- What is your definition of power? Do you feel powerful? What can you do to be more powerful in your life?

- What do you need to do to deepen your trust in the Universe? Are you showing up and doing your part?

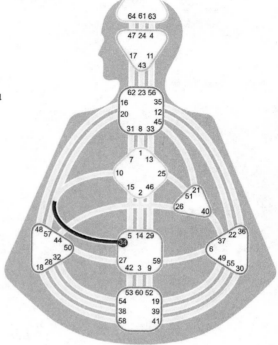

Figure 95: Gate 34.

Affirmation

I trust the Universe to deliver to me the perfect opportunities to fulfill my dreams and intentions. I watch and wait for signs that clearly show me the next step. I know that my true power is in cocreation with the Universe, and I know that when I wait, the right opportunity to use my power to create will be revealed.

Gate 35: Change

I Ching: Progress

> *Theme:* You know which experiences are worthy and worthwhile. You partake in the right experiences and share your knowledge for the sake of changing the story of what's possible in the world.

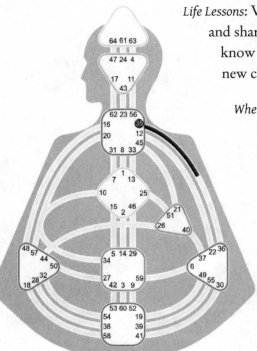

Figure 96: Gate 35.

Life Lessons: Value your own wisdom and experience, and share your story with others. Trust that you know how to face and embrace change and new circumstances with grace.

When Unbalanced: You might be jaded and unwilling to try new things. You might not value your own experience and fail to share what you know with others.

Contemplation

- What is going on in your life right now that you would like to change?

- In your current manifestations, what experiences would you like to avoid duplicating? How can that understanding help you get clear about your creation? What experiences do you need to focus and align with?

Affirmation

I choose the kinds of experiences I desire. My feelings about my experiences show me what is correct for me. I am responsible for my own choices and my own happiness, and no one can create experiences for me that I do not choose.

Gate 36: Crisis

I Ching: The Darkening of the Light

Theme: You take bold new actions that break old patterns and change the story and expectations of what is possible.

Life Lessons: Wait for the right timing to try something new. Don't let old patterns and habits keep you from doing what you feel passionate about. Make the seemingly impossible possible.

When Unbalanced: You might let boredom cause you to leap into chaos without preparing for the experience.

Contemplation

- What is your strategy for coping with unexpected events, chaos, and tragedy?

- How strong is your connection to Spirit? What could you do to strengthen it?

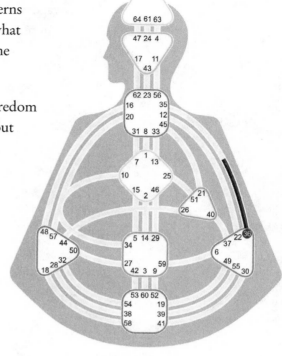

Figure 97: Gate 36.

Affirmation

I embrace the new. I watch and wait. I trust my intuition and my Strategy, knowing that I make clear, intentional choices. My action are in alignment with my intentions and my desires. I am the eye of the storm. My head is clear, my heart is aligned, and I only act for my highest good. I am immune to the appearances of my outer reality, and I know that I am on my way to creating what I intend. My beliefs are unwavering; I am not swayed by outer circumstances. I trust in divine order.

Gate 37: Friendship
I Ching: The Family

Theme: You stay connected to sustainable peace and respond to life by making peaceful choices no matter what's going on in the world.

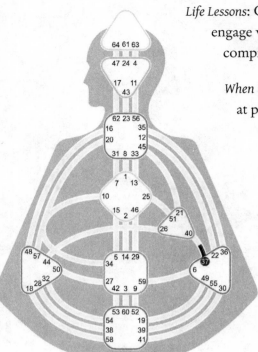

Life Lessons: Cultivate a sense of inner peace and engage with others from that place without compromising your value or theirs.

When Unbalanced: You might struggle to be at peace. You might repress emotions that don't feel peaceful or be conflict avoidant.

Figure 98: Gate 37.

Contemplation

• What areas of your life are in need of peace right now? What are five peace-enhancing activities you could do for yourself?

• What new kinds of agreements do you need to make with your partners? Are your agreements clear? Do all parties have the same expectations?

Affirmation

There is always calm after the storm. It is in the quietness that follows shift and change that I remember my bearings, breathe deeply, and realign my relationships with what is new. All agreements I make are clear and created with peace as the end goal. From the remnants of the past, I discover the blessings and I work with my friends, family, community, and world to cocreate a mutually respectful and deeply honoring peace. Peace is within me. I am peace. I breathe peace. I create peace and all is well.

Gate 38: The Fighter

I Ching: Opposition

Theme: You know what's worth committing to and fighting for, and you use your experiences to craft a vision that anchors the possibility of something truly meaningful and worthy in the world. You serve the world as a visionary.

Life Lessons: Do not let struggle and challenge cause you to quit your dream.

When Unbalanced: You might struggle and fight without direction, and be oppositional to a fault. You might fail to cultivate a dream and feel lost.

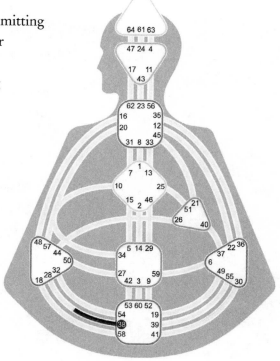

Figure 99: Gate 38.

Contemplation

- Do you know what's worth committing to and fighting for in your life?

- Do you have a dream that you are sharing with the world?

- Do you know how to use your struggles and challenges as the catalyst for creating deeper meaning in the world? In your life?

Affirmation

I have deep clarity about my life purpose and direction. Serving my purpose inspires me and gives me the energy to take powerful steps forward in my life, no matter what comes my way.

I am here for a unique purpose, and I honor that by setting clear intentions and taking actions that reflect that purpose.

Gate 39: Provocation

I Ching: Obstruction

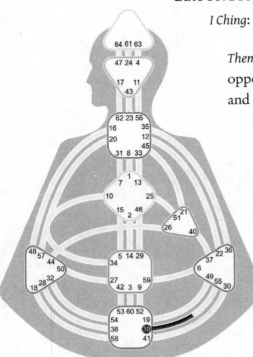

Theme: You can transform an experience into an opportunity. You see and experience scarcity and can use this awareness to recalibrate your energy toward sufficiency and abundance.

Life Lessons: Speak your truth in a measured and appropriate way.

When Unbalanced: You might challenge others purely for the sake of being provocative or to get inappropriate attention.

Contemplation

- Can you think of a time when the moment felt right and a correct manifestation followed? How did you feel?

Figure 100: Gate 39.

- Do you push people and opportunities away?

- Do you speak your truth with confidence? Do you value your insights enough to wait for the right timing and receptivity?

Affirmation

I wait for the right spirit of things before I progress. I take my time and allow the right doors to open to pathways that place me in the right place, at the right time, doing the right thing. I speak my truth when I see others not living true to their value and values.

Gate 40: Loneliness

I Ching: Deliverance

Theme: You retreat as a way of replenishing your inner and outer resources and bring your renewed self back into community when you are ready.

Life Lessons: Rest appropriately; know when you need to retreat for the sake of self-renewal.

When Unbalanced: You might fail to take a break and rest, pushing too hard and burning out. You might try to prove your value by overdoing for others.

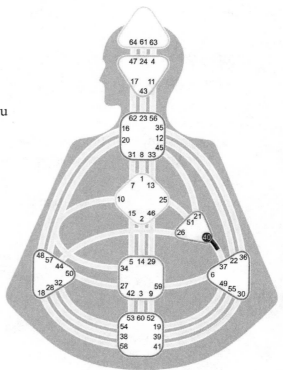

Figure 101: Gate 40.

Contemplation

- What is the nature of your relationships? Do you feel lonely? Do your relationships feel balanced?

- Do you need to make more connections with others? Network? Join social groups?

- Are you doing enough to maintain your energy? Are you taking the time you need to care for yourself?

Affirmation

I am deeply connected to my need for retreat and renewal. I know that self-care and self-renewal are essential for me to serve the world and my loved ones at my highest level. I allow myself the time I need to recalibrate my energy before I commit to nurturing others. Staying in alignment with my own energy helps me hold true to my agreements and commitments.

Gate 41: Fantasy

I Ching: Decrease

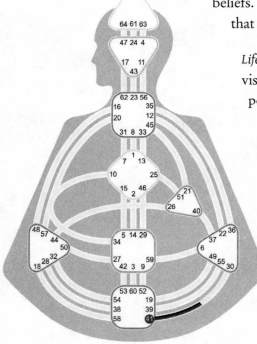

Figure 102: Gate 41.

Theme: You use your imagination to generate ideas about new abundant opportunities in the world. You sustain these abundant visions, share them when necessary, and break old patterns and limiting beliefs. You are able to hold the vision of a miracle that transcends expectations.

Life Lessons: Use your imagination and visualization to stay inspired and in a state of positive expectation. Recognize the difference between imagination and possibility versus fantasy.

When Unbalanced: You might live in fantasy and fail to see reality. You might lose faith because your fantasies don't come true.

Contemplation

• What do you need to do to deepen your connection with Spirit? Do you feel aligned with something bigger than yourself? Do you need to create a routine to stay centered and connected?

• Are you giving yourself enough time to explore your imagination and creativity?

Affirmation

In the stillness I surrender to the great mystery of life and the Divine. I allow divine inspiration to wash over me, and I listen with great attention and appreciation. I trust that I receive the perfect inspiration and simply let the inspiration flow. I am grateful.

Gate 42: Finishing Things

I Ching: Increase

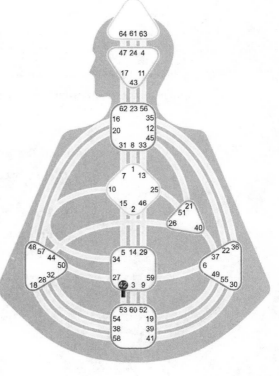

Theme: You respond to being inserted into opportunities, experiences, and events that you have the wisdom to facilitate and complete. You know exactly what needs to be done to create space for something new.

Life Lessons: Let go. Trust that sometimes you have to finish one thing before you can begin something new. Do the work necessary to bring things to a healthy conclusion.

Figure 103: Gate 42.

When Unbalanced: You might fail to finish things and create a backlog that needs to be completed to create room for something new. You might look so far into the future that it becomes hard to start something new. You might bring things to a close prematurely, keeping you from going deep enough to achieve mastery.

Contemplation

- What final steps do you need to take to release the energy of old situations or relationships? What doors do you see opening? Closing?

- Are there any situations or circumstances in your life that need to be finished up to make room for something new?

Affirmation

I embrace all the change that has come before, and I recognize that all endings are new beginnings. I open the door for the new and redream what is to come. I am fully prepared to lay down the physical manifestation of what is new and to take the actions necessary to bring what is new into form.

Gate 43: Insight

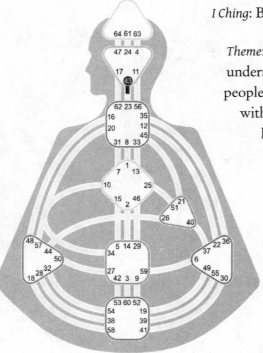

I Ching: Breakthrough

Theme: You tap in to new knowledge, understandings, and insights that expand people's understanding of the world. You align with the right timing and trust that you'll know how to share what you know when you need to share it.

Life Lessons: Trust epiphanies and deep inner knowing.

When Unbalanced: You might tell people about your new transformative ideas before they are ready to hear them or before you can clearly articulate them.

Figure 104: Gate 43.

Contemplation

- What are all your current thoughts, ideas, and inspirations?

- Can you see a pattern of something new emerging? Are you on the cusp of a breakthrough?

Affirmation

I take time to enjoy my thoughts. I allow myself to begin to formulate new ideas and inspirations that can create change in my life and in the lives of others. I recognize and allow for my own brilliance and serve this brilliance by waiting for the right people to ask me for my insights. My thoughts and ideas are valuable, and I trust that what I have to share is valuable to the right people. I attract the right support, circumstances, and opportunities that align with my new ideas.

Gate 44: Energy
I Ching: Coming to Meet

Theme: You can see patterns that have created pain and bring awareness to help yourself and others break old patterns and transform that pain into value and alignment with purpose.

Life Lessons: Use your intuitive understanding of the patterns of the past to help others or yourself. Transform the lessons of the past into something of greater value and use this understanding to deepen integrity and create more value.

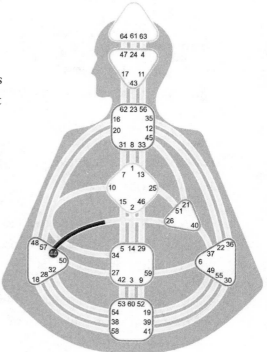

Figure 105: Gate 44.

When Unbalanced: You might be afraid that the past will repeat itself and let this fear keep you stuck or blocked from forward momentum.

Contemplation

- Are there places where you limit yourself because of things that have happened to you in the past?

- Are you in full integrity when it comes to leading or influencing others? Do you walk your talk?

- Are there places where you need support from others?

- Imagine your perception of your life from your deathbed. What things would be important to you? What accomplishments would you be most proud of? Is your life today a good reflection of that perspective? Do you need to change your priorities?

Affirmation

I greet life full-on. I move forward confidently knowing that my past has been my greatest teacher. I am not limited but liberated from my past and realize that now is the most powerful moment of my life.

Gate 45: The King or Queen

I Ching: Gathering Together

Theme: You understand that knowledge and material resources are powerful, and know how to use both to sustain others and help them grow their own abundant foundation.

Life Lessons: Use your natural ability to lead in service to others. Assess the resources and information available and find a path to equitably share or teach.

When Unbalanced: You might lead with ego, take more than your fair share out of fear of scarcity, or embody diva energy as a way of overcompensating for an internal lack of self-worth.

Contemplation

- Where in your life do you need to assume a leadership role? How do you feel as a leader? Is it okay for you to be in charge, honor your creation, and speak your truth?

- What do you need to do to attract the right people into your life to serve your manifestation and creation? Is your mindset aligned with being a team player?

- Are there places where you need to let go of your creation and allow it to evolve?

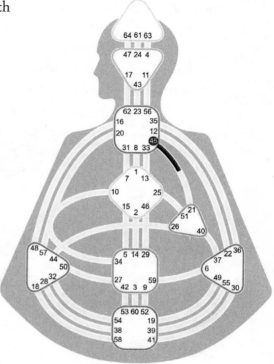

Figure 106: Gate 45.

Affirmation

I gather all the people necessary to support my manifestation in my life. I take leadership and honor my role as the king/queen of my creation. I assert my power, delegate, manage resources effectively, and act with benevolence.

Gate 46: Love of Body

I Ching: Pushing Upward

Theme: You recognize that the body is the vehicle for the soul and love the body as a vital element of the soul's expression in life. You nurture, are grounded in, and fully care for the body. You savor the physicality of the human experience and explore how to fully embody Spirit in your body. You are committed to seeing how much life force you can embody in your physical form.

Life Lessons: Love and take care of your body. Appreciate the body as a servant to the soul.

When Unbalanced: You might hate your body, fail to be in your body, or neglect or ignore the messages your body is giving you.

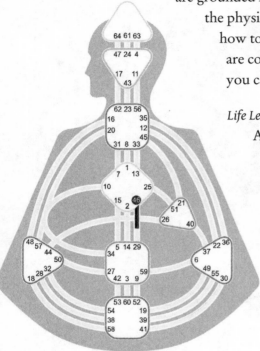

Figure 107: Gate 46.

Contemplation

• What is your reality telling you? Are there messages you need to heed?

• What discourages you? Do you push or do you allow? What do you need to do to allow rather than think your way through something?

• How can you love your body more? How can you take better care of your body?

Affirmation

Physical reality is an expression of my consciousness. I look to my reality to mirror my mindset and my beliefs back to me. I am clear, conscious, and awake. I am aware that I can adjust my mindset to create any physical experience I choose. I take guided actions that are in alignment with my beliefs, and I celebrate this gift of being alive in a physical body.

Gate 47: Realization

I Ching: Oppression

Theme: You engage in hopeful, inspired thoughts no matter what is going on around you. You use inspiration as a catalyst for calibrating emotional frequency and the heart.

Life Lessons: Harness the power of hope and positive expectations. Trust that the answers to your questions and the solutions to your inspirations will appear; wait for and trust in an epiphany.

When Unbalanced: You might let a negative mindset and despair keep you from seeing possible solutions.

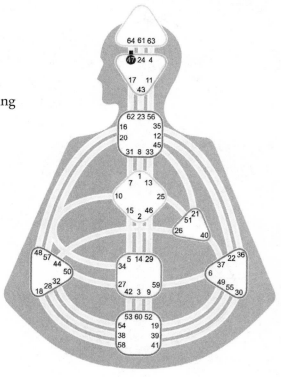

Figure 108: Gate 47.

Contemplation

- What things will you do while you are waiting for your manifestation? What will you do to keep your vibration high while you wait?

- What is the status of your mindset? Do you need to take care of your thought patterns?

Affirmation

I wait with delighted anticipation and marvel at the curious way the Universe manifests my desires. I keep my mindset joyful and positive, and I only focus on the end result.

Gate 48: Depth

I Ching: The Well

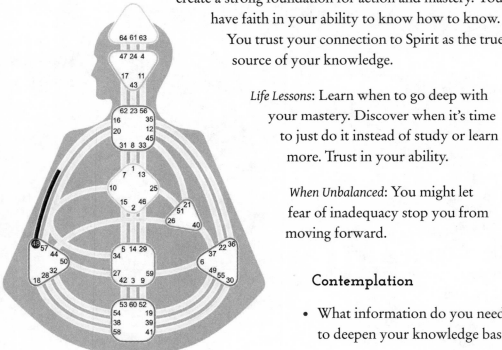

Theme: You have the wisdom and the depth of knowledge necessary to create a strong foundation for action and mastery. You have faith in your ability to know how to know. You trust your connection to Spirit as the true source of your knowledge.

Life Lessons: Learn when to go deep with your mastery. Discover when it's time to just do it instead of study or learn more. Trust in your ability.

When Unbalanced: You might let fear of inadequacy stop you from moving forward.

Figure 109: Gate 48.

Contemplation

- What information do you need to deepen your knowledge base?

- Do you have the skills necessary to bring forth what you desire? If not, what do you need to master?

Affirmation

I trust that the skills I need will be expressed through me when I am ready. I study. I learn. I know that my knowledge will be beautifully expressed when the time and circumstances are correct. I trust in divine order.

Gate 49: Principles

I Ching: Revolution

Theme: You can sense when it's time to align with a higher value. You inspire others to make expansive changes that embrace higher principles and a deeper alignment with peace and sustainability.

Life Lessons: Intimacy and relationships need to evolve to stay supportive and expansive. Do the work by being willing to renegotiate the agreements of partnership to reflect shifts and changes in values. Hold true to your value and the value of your partner and act in alignment with your self-worth.

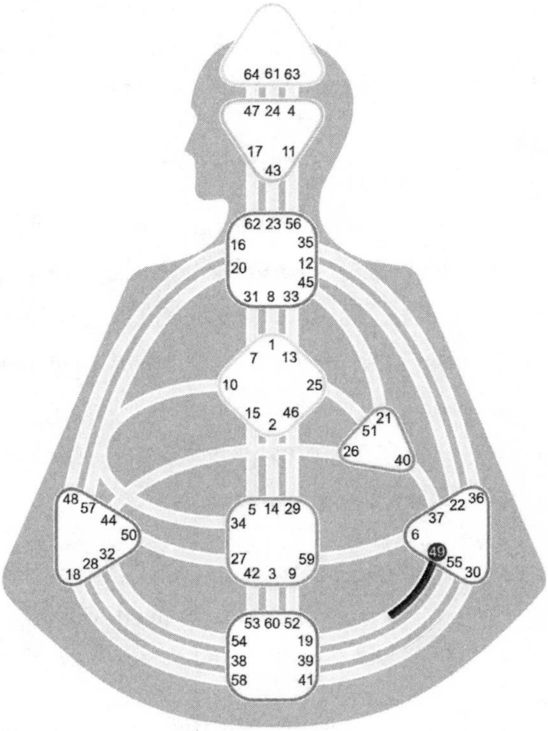

Figure 110: Gate 49.

When Unbalanced: You might fail to change the agreement in a relationship when you feel devalued or like your values have changed. You might hold on for too long. You might be so afraid of negotiating that you cultivate a pattern of quitting or leaving too quickly without giving your relationship a chance to evolve or grow.

Contemplation

- What actions do you need to take to make room for love in your life? What conversations do you need to have? What agreements do you need to change?

- Are there actions that you need to take to express your love and appreciation more deeply? Are there places where you need to create more honoring, understanding, and respect for your partners?

- What actions do you need to take to start a transformational revolution in your life? What habits, intentions, and desires need to be anchored in your reality?

Affirmation

After contemplation and alignment, I now take guided actions to revolutionize my life. I know exactly the actions to take to create lasting change and transformation in my life. I am empowered. My choices and actions are deliberate. I am ready to redefine and recreate all agreements in my life to align with the truth of my unlimited abundance.

Gate 50: Values

I Ching: The Cauldron

> *Theme*: You nurture yourself so that you have more to give others. You know what others need to bring them into greater alignment with love, and you share what you have to increase the well-being of others.

> *Life Lessons*: Nurture in an empowering way; don't deplete yourself in the name of caring for others, and don't let your fear of letting other people down or their suffering the consequences of their own actions cause you to overcompensate or feel guilty.

When Unbalanced: You might overnurture to the point of burnout, care to the point of overtaking. You might let guilt cause you to make commitments that don't feel good or aligned.

Contemplation

- Do you need to create new rules in your relationships, business, health, wealth, and welfare?

- Do you love yourself? Do you need to nurture yourself more? Do you have the strength and foundation to love freely? Do you feel safe in love?

Affirmation

I establish the rules for my reality. I take care and nourish myself so that I may take care and nourish others. Everything I do for others I do for myself first to sustain my energy and power. I rule with self-love and then love freely.

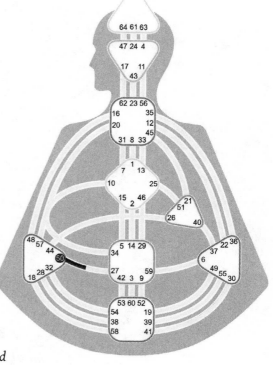

Figure 111: Gate 50.

Gate 51: Shock
I Ching: The Arousing

Theme: You consciously use cycles of disruption and unexpected twists and turns of faith to deepen your connection to Spirit and to your life and soul purpose.

Life Lessons: Be resilient and pivot in the face of the unexpected. Don't let the unexpected cause you to lose faith; use your personal challenges to help awaken others to hope and possibility.

When Unbalanced: You might use shock or be shocking as a way of getting attention. You might let the unexpected cause you to lose faith and direction. You might get stuck on trying to go back to how things were before an unexpected shift and change.

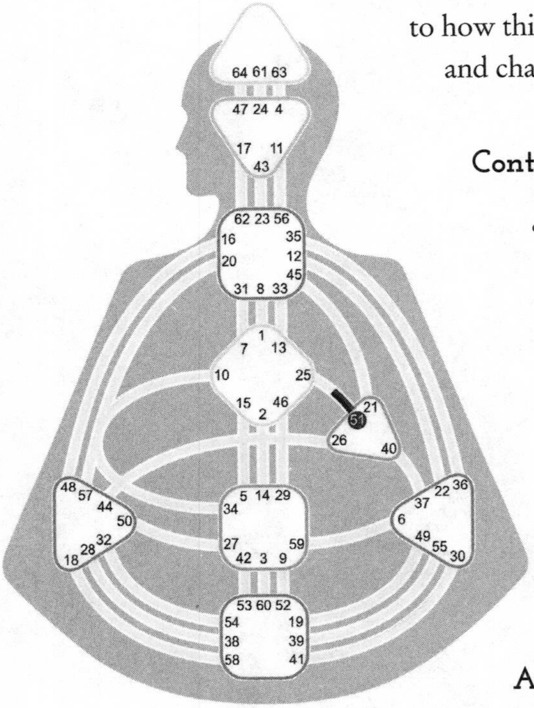

Figure 112: Gate 51.

Contemplation

- What lessons have you learned from shock? How have you transformed shock into truth and strength? How has shock initiated you into the love of Spirit?

- What trauma and drama do you need to release? What do you need to do to move into gratitude?

Affirmation

I have the inner strength to deflect all outer shock. I am the manifestation of Spirit in form. I am courageous, steadfast, and open to the expansion of Spirit within me. My faith and courage inspire and initiate others. My vibration is high, and I lift others up with the truth of Spirit within me.

Gate 52: Stillness

I Ching: Keeping Still (Mountain)

Theme: You see the bigger picture and purpose of what is going on around you and know exactly where to focus your energy and attention to facilitate the unfolding of what's to come.

Life Lessons: Take a step back while staying focused on the long-term goal. Listen attentively to your own inner wisdom and follow your Human Design Strategy and Authority to determine where to put your focus.

When Unbalanced: You might get so deep in the details of an inconsequential factor that you lose momentum.

Contemplation

- What do you do to maintain your focus? Is there anything in your environment or your life that you need to move out of the way for you to deepen your focus?

- How do you manage being overwhelmed? What things are you avoiding because you feel overwhelmed by them? What is one bold action you can take to clear the path for action?

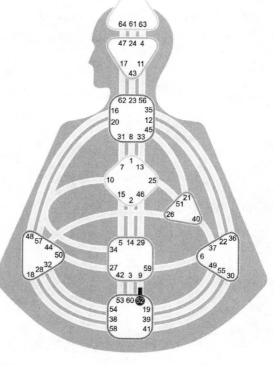

Figure 113: Gate 52.

- How does your overwhelm affect your self-worth? How can you love yourself more deeply despite being overwhelmed?

Affirmation

The stillness of my concentration allows patterns and order to be revealed to me. My understanding of this order gives me the power to continue to create effectively. The stillness of my concentration is the spirit of my power this week.

Gate 53: Starting Things

I Ching: Development

Theme: You sit with inspiration and are attuned to what the inspiration wants and needs. You launch the initiation sequence for an idea, and then let the idea follow its right course with trust in the flow.

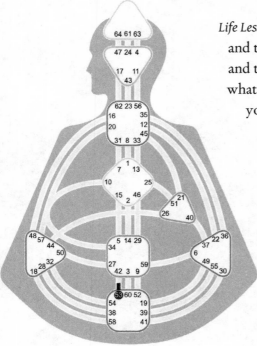

Life Lessons: Learn which ideas are yours to start, and trust that you'll attract the right people and the right parameters to help accomplish what you set out to do. Be gentle with yourself if you don't always finish projects; give yourself permission to learn from the process. See your ability to begin something as your gift, not your weakness.

When Unbalanced: You might feel desperate or frenetic about bringing all your ideas to fruition. You might beat yourself up for not finishing what you've started, or feel shame or guilt whenever you can't follow through.

Figure 114: Gate 53.

Contemplation

- What messages did you receive growing up about finishing things? How have those messages shaped your perception of your ability to start things?

- What needs to be healed, released, aligned, or brought to your awareness for you to embrace your gift of being good at starting things?

Affirmation

I wait and start things according to my Strategy. I allow for the energy of new beginnings and trust that when I live my Strategy, all the key pieces to complete my creative process will magically align.

Gate 54: Drive

I Ching: The Marrying Maiden

Theme: You cultivate a deep relationship with inspiration and prepare the way for an idea to become reality by aligning it energetically and laying foundational action.

Life Lessons: Take daily action to keep momentum flowing. Make sure that the foundation of what you want to create is laid so that when the time is right it's easy for an idea to come to fruition. Master endurance and trust in right timing.

When Unbalanced: You might hold on to an idea but fail to do the work associated with it. You might quit before you have prepared the way.

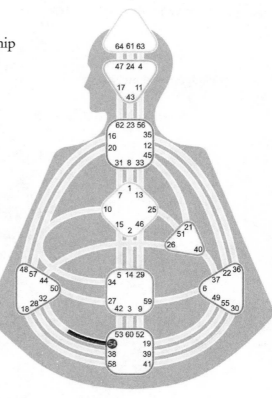

Figure 115: Gate 54.

Contemplation

- What actions do you need to take that will show yourself and the Universe that you are ready for action?

- What positive steps will you take toward your dreams?

Affirmation

I am clear. I am focused. I am ready to do whatever it takes to make my dreams come true. I know that my clarity married with my aligned actions are the perfect energies necessary to create miracles in my world. I am noticed, heard, seen, and recognized for what I have to offer, and the Universe perfectly conspires with me to make magic happen and my dreams come true.

Gate 55: Spirit

I Ching: Abundance

Theme: You hold the emotional frequency of energy and the vision for a creation. You trust in sufficiency so deeply that you're able to create without limitation.

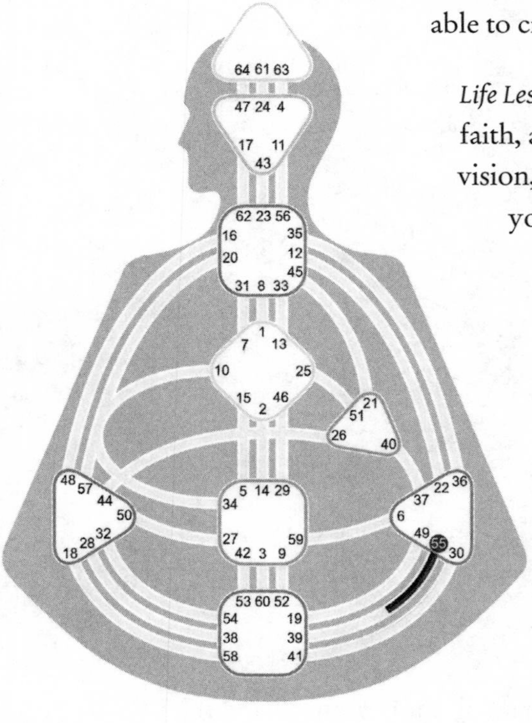

Life Lessons: Cultivate an attitude of patience, faith, and positive expectation. Hold the vision, no matter what is happening around you or despite a lack of evidence that your vision is coming to fruition. Trust in abundance and sufficiency.

When Unbalanced: You might leap from thing to thing because you don't have faith or value yourself enough to believe that you are worthy of a positive outcome.

Contemplation

- What do you need to do to release any worries and fears that you may

Figure 116: Gate 55.

THE HUMAN DESIGN WORKBOOK

have about abundance in your life? What beliefs do you have about being fully supported and abundant? Do you need to align these beliefs with what you know is true?

- What does being aware of the abundance of Spirit within you feel like? What does it look like? How would being constantly aware of this fulfilling energy change your life? What do you need to do to be ready for this level of faith and trust?

Affirmation

I am aware of the abundance of Spirit within me. I know that when I am focused on this abundance in Spirit all my desires are fulfilled, and it is impossible for me to experience lack or need. I am completely supported and fulfilled by this awareness. By letting go and letting God, I allow abundance in all aspects of my life to manifest fully for me. Abundance is my birthright and my natural state.

Gate 56: The Storyteller
I Ching: The Wanderer

Theme: You share stories that stimulate expansive, possibility-oriented thinking and powerful emotional energy that creates evolution and growth.

Life Lessons: Wait to share your insights, stories, and metaphors with those who are ready to receive your wisdom.

When Unbalanced: You might fail to wait for the right audience or the receptivity of others. You might hold on to old stories that are limiting or fail to be expansive enough to help you or others grow.

Contemplation

- What stories do you share repeatedly with others? Do they lift people up or cause them to contract?

- What stories do you tell about yourself and your voice that cause you to either expand or contract?

- What are you here to inspire others to do or be?

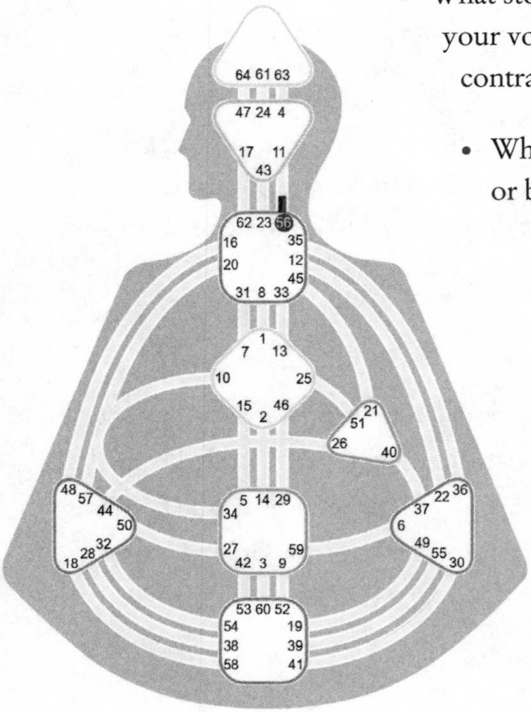

Affirmation

I wait to share my ideas and my sacred stories when I am asked by the right people who honor my inspiration and experience. Stories are the vehicle to growing the tapestry of humanity. My story is an important part of the human experience, and I honor my experience by waiting for the right circumstances. My words and my dreams are valuable.

Figure 117: Gate 56.

Gate 57: Intuition
I Ching: The Gentle

Theme: You sense when it is the right time to act. You intuitively know what needs to be prepared for the future and follow through on it.

Life Lessons: Trust your intuition and the right timing to share your insights.

When Unbalanced: You might be afraid of the future, doubt your intuitive knowing, or blurt out your knowingness without respect for timing.

Contemplation

- What does your intuition feel like? What might you do to deepen your intuitive awareness?

- When have you trusted your intuition and things worked out well?

- Are there any intuitive hunches you are receiving right now that need attention?

Affirmation

I trust myself. I trust my intuition. I trust the future.

Gate 58: Joy

I Ching: Joy

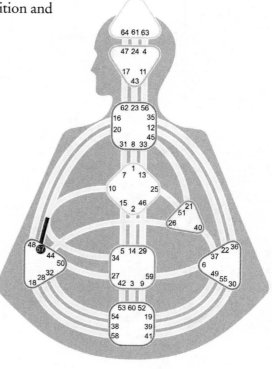

Figure 118: Gate 57.

Theme: You harness the joy of mastery and refine your practice until you fulfill your potential. You live in the flow of joy.

Life Lessons: Do not compromise on what brings you joy.

When Unbalanced: You might compromise on doing what brings you joy, forcing yourself to try to master something you dislike and losing your zest for life.

Contemplation

- What are you grateful for?

- Can you try taking a few minutes to stay in that place of blissful appreciation every day this week?

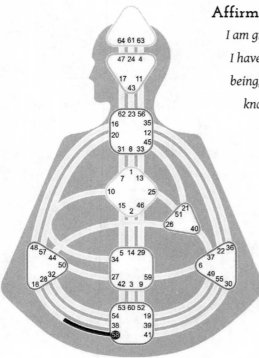

Figure 119: Gate 58.

Affirmation

I am grateful for everything that I am, that I have, and that I have experienced. I allow joy to permeate every cell of my being, and I stand in awe of all my blessings. I relax and know that the shower of blessings, which is my life, is part of my divine heritage, and I relax knowing that an endless stream of good flows toward me.

Gate 59: Sexuality

I Ching: Dispersion

Theme: You trust in sufficiency and know that when you create abundance there is great fulfillment in sharing. You craft partnerships and relationships with others that sustain you and the foundation of your lives.

Life Lessons: Trust that there is enough, and share what you have without depleting yourself. Do work creating sustainable resources for others; help take care of the people you love.

When Unbalanced: You might manipulate, steal, or overcompensate for a perceived lack of resources. You might fight or hoard because you fail to believe in sufficiency. You might defend the belief that there isn't enough.

Contemplation

- What avenues of impact would best serve you, your intentions, and your business?

- What is the next step in creating your intentions and your dreams? Where do you need to get to work to be ready for things to manifest?

Affirmation

I radiate my desires and dreams into the Universe. My intentions influence the right people, the right places, the right circumstances, and the right opportunities at the perfect time, and I know that I am radiating pure joyful intention all the time.

Gate 60: Acceptance

I Ching: Limitation

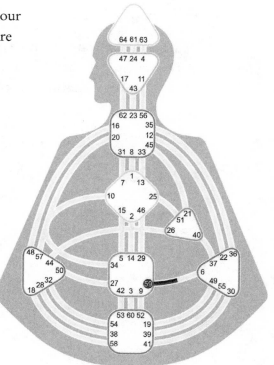

Figure 120: Gate 59.

Theme: You find the blessings in transformation. You're optimistic and know how to focus on what is working instead of what's not.

Life Lessons: Use gratitude as a gateway for innovation. Be highly adaptable by virtue of appreciating what you have. Know that you truly cannot change an experience that you hate. Let go of your old, fixed ideas and embrace the new.

When Unbalanced: You might be ungrateful and bitter and focus on what you don't have as opposed to what you do. You might hold on to old ideas so tightly that you can't see innovative options in front of you.

Contemplation

- What things might you need to conserve for the sake of the future? Do you need to change your financial, relationship, health, work, or spiritual habits? If so, how?

- Are there any old habits, circumstances, or situations that you need to release to support you in aligning your energy?

- Do you need to improve your focus to gain momentum? If so, what changes in your daily habits would help?

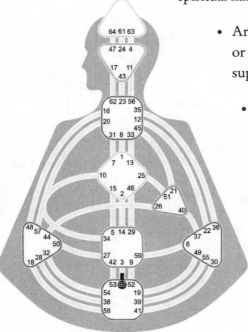

Figure 121: Gate 60.

Affirmation

I am committed to creating a life that is in alignment with my dreams. I courageously release anything that no longer serves me and conserve my resources wisely. I know that I am fully supported and that I have been given everything I need to move forward in a powerful way.

Gate 61: Mystery
I Ching: Inner Truth

Theme: You see purpose in a bigger perspective that transcends the smaller details of an experience or event. You stay in a state of innocence and delusional confidence as a way of sustaining powerful creativity.

Life Lessons: Embrace the idea that everything happens for a reason. Even painful events can be catalytic if you allow yourself to find the blessings in the pain.

When Unbalanced: You might get so lost in the question of why an experience happened that you can't see the blessings in the pain or find a practical way forward.

Contemplation

- What do you do to maintain your sense of wonder? How can you deepen your awe of the magnificence of the Universe?

- What old thoughts, patterns, and beliefs do you need to release to align with your knowingness and to trust your "delusional confidence" as a powerful creative state?

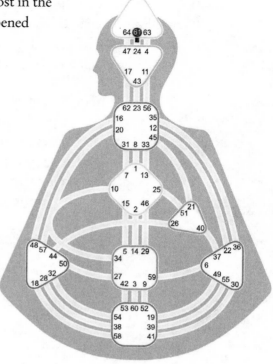

Figure 122: Gate 61.

Affirmation

In the stillness, I surrender to the great mystery of life and the Divine. I allow divine inspiration to wash over me, and I listen with great attention and appreciation. I trust that I receive the perfect inspiration and simply let the inspiration flow to me. I am grateful.

Gate 62: Details

I Ching: The Preponderance of the Small

> *Theme*: You are tuned in to what is necessary to be prepared and trust that your alignment will inform you of everything that you need.

Life Lessons: Master the process of being prepared and trust that your knowledge of how to be ready and how to pivot is the only thing you need to know. Glean enough experience to trust you'll know what you need to know when you need to know it.

When Unbalanced: You might let worry cause you to expend exhausting amounts of energy being ready for all possible outcomes, including worst-case scenarios.

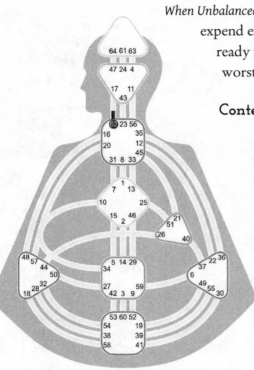

Figure 123: Gate 62.

Contemplation

- Do you have anxiety? What do you do to manage your anxiety?

- What can you do to trust that you know what you need to know? What proof do you have that you are in the flow of preparation?

Affirmation

I use my words carefully. My words generate form for my dreams and ideas. My thoughts are clear and organized, and I find and speak the truth with courage and consistency.

Gate 63: Doubt

I Ching: After Completion

Theme: You use curiosity as a way of stimulating dreams of new possibilities and potentials. Your thoughts inspire the question of what needs to happen to make an idea a reality.

Life Lessons: Create from a place of curiosity and open-mindedness. Be comfortable with thinking about possibilities without having to figure it out. Learn to trust that, with time and conscious contemplation, the answers will prove themselves to be true or not. Remember that your ideas need to be experimented with before you know whether they are correct or not.

When Unbalanced: You might embrace your ideas as certain truth. You might fail to question ideas, or question ideas so profoundly that you begin to doubt yourself and your creative insights.

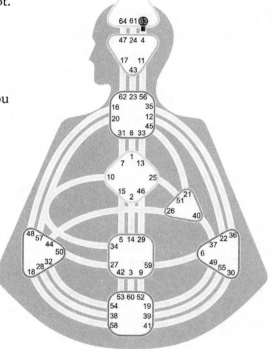

Figure 124: Gate 63.

Contemplation

- What experiences have you had that have caused you to doubt yourself? What do you need to do to release your self-doubt, to forgive the mistakes?

- What experiences have you had that have shown you that your inner knowingness is correct?

- What are your gifts, strengths, and talents? Where have you demonstrated mastery?

- Do you trust in divine order? What mistakes have you witnessed that ultimately created a path to perfection and mastery? What could you do to integrate mistakes as a crucial part of mastery?

Affirmation

I trust myself. I trust the Divine. I trust that there is perfection in experimentation. I trust my insight and knowingness. I am discerning but not doubtful. I know that all questions have answers. I trust in the elegant solution and know that the answer will be mine in time and all is well.

Gate 64: Confusion

I Ching: Before Completion

Theme: You receive a big idea and serve the idea by giving it your imagination and dreaming. You trust that you'll know how to implement the idea if it is yours to make manifest; to hold the energy of an idea for the world.

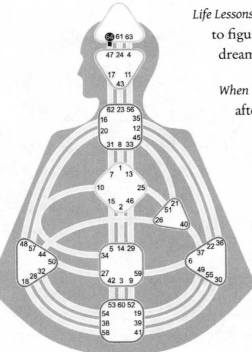

Life Lessons: Be patient and wait for the epiphany to figure out the how of your big ideas and dreams. Trust the process.

When Unbalanced: You might follow idea after idea and pressure yourself to figure out how to make them come true. You might quit or discount your ideas when you can't figure them out, and let your impatience cause you to doubt your creativity and inspiration.

Contemplation

- What are your big dreams? Do you trust that they will manifest?

Figure 125: Gate 64.

- What strategies do you have to stay in joy while you wait for your manifestation?

- Can you spend some time away from human information sources? Go for a walk or a hike? What answers does nature offer you, if you're able to get out there and rest your brain?

Affirmation

I pay attention to inspiration and know that when I wait with curious anticipation to see how my inspiration manifests, I am delighted and curious to see what the Universe brings.

Working with the Planets and Gates

Look for which Gates your planets occupy in your chart. As you find each piece of information, insert it into the appropriate spot in the statement template below. (Note: Different chart software may present the planets in a different order, so be sure to double-check that you are placing the correct information into the template.)

I powerfully and passionately declare that my life purpose is to:
_____ (conscious Sun ☉ Gate theme)
and _____ (unconscious Sun ☉ Gate theme).

To do this, I allow, create, and receive _____ (conscious Earth ⊕ theme) and _____ (unconscious Earth ⊕ theme) as part of the foundation of the deep well of creativity that I am.

My early life experience brings me opportunities to learn and embrace
_____ (South Node ☋ —Personality Gate theme)
and _____ (South Node ☋ —Design Gate theme).

I look forward to keeping these lessons and experiences to help me fully lean into
_____ (North Node ☊ —Personality Gate theme) and
_____ (North Node ☊ —Design Gate theme), as I
mature in my essence and expression around age forty-four. I know the Universe
brings me opportunities so that I may learn to embrace and love all parts of me,
and I align with my essence as I grow, learn, and share with the world.

My heart and soul are driven by _____ (conscious
Moon ☽ Gate theme) and _____ (unconscious Moon
☽ Gate theme). I know that nurturing this drive gives me the energy and passion
to continue to align myself with my purpose. I embrace the challenge as part of
my learning and growth process. I know that when I encounter an inner conflict,
it is a symptom of my own expansion and indicates that I am learning and growing. I am always doing it right. I am always growing and changing.

My personal learning energy teaches me _____
(Saturn ♄ —Personality Gate theme) and _____
(Saturn ♄ —Design Gate theme).

When I master my inner lessons, I am blessed by _____
(Jupiter ♃ —Personality Gate theme) and _____
(Jupiter ♃ —Design Gate theme).

My spiritual purpose and path is _____
(Neptune ♆ —Personality Gate theme) and _____
(Neptune ♆ —Design Gate theme).

I call on these energies when I am in need of greater alignment with my Purpose.
I know that I need to master _____
(Chiron ⚷ —Personality Gate theme) and _____
(Chiron ⚷ —Design Gate theme) to deepen what I am here to share with the world.

I use this knowledge and wisdom to communicate through _____
_____ (Mercury ☿ —Personality Gate theme) and
_____ (Mercury ☿ —Design Gate theme).

I value _____ (conscious Venus ♀)
and _____ (unconscious Venus ♀).

My life lessons have taught me that I'm willing to fight for_____
_____(conscious Mars ♂) and _____
_____ (unconscious Mars ♂).

I was born into a generation that will awaken others to _____
_____ (conscious Uranus ♅) and _____
(unconscious Uranus ♅).

And will learn these lessons through cycles of _____
(conscious and unconscious Pluto ♇).

I share the full expression of who I am with the world through these energies. I play a unique role in the evolution of humanity, and I have a vital and irreplaceable place in the divine order. I honor all of who I am, and I deeply and completely love and accept myself.

Epilogue

PUTTING IT ALL TOGETHER

Between stimulus and response there is a space. In that space is our
power to choose our response. In our response lies our growth and our freedom.
—Viktor E. Frankl

Throughout this book, we've explored who you are and how your unique energy blueprint influences how you interact with and experience the world around you. The purpose of understanding this information is that it helps you remember who you are—who you were born to be—and how to begin living a life that is aligned with that original intention.

You are a once-in-a-lifetime cosmic event. There has never been and never will be anyone like you again.

You're also an irreplaceable, unique, and vital part of the cosmic plan. The world is what it is because of you. If you weren't part of the world, the world wouldn't be what it is today.

Human Design gives us tools to help us fulfill our right place and take up our right space in the world. But there's more to the Human Design story than using Human Design as a tool to help you actualize your potential. The chart also tells us a story of how to fulfill the potential of humanity. It gives us deep insights into

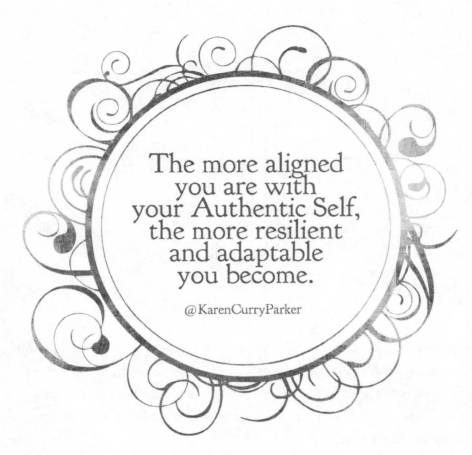

Figure 126: Personal Alignment.

how our unique lives are not only important to us individually but are essential parts of the human story.

Human Design isn't just a personality assessment tool. The story of Human Design is revealed wisdom—information given to the founder of the Human Design System, Ra Uru Hu, over the course of eight days in January 1987. During the transmission of the body of knowledge that would become the Human Design System, Ra was told that we are on the edge of a big evolutionary leap in the human story. The Human Design chart itself is changing, giving us new hardwiring—an upgraded energy blueprint—that will help humanity fulfill its destiny as abundant, sustainable, equitable, just, and peaceful beings.

I believe that we are all here on the planet at this vital time because we are collectively ushering in a new era of peace. You play a vital role in birthing this new expression of humanity.

There is a space between stimulus and response. The story you tell about who you are lives in that space. To create a better world, we have to take back control over that space and our stories. Learning how to regain power of the story you tell about who you are is essential to helping you learn how to stop reacting to life and start deliberating and intentionally creating your life.

The greatest work we must do at this time is to decondition ourselves. We must untangle ourselves from all the old limiting stories that run the world and our individual lives. The very first step in creating a new world and ushering in a new consciousness on the planet is to reframe the stories we tell about who we are.

If the story you tell about yourself is one that devalues who you are, limits your potential, pushes you into the box of society's expectations, and causes you to be a victim of your destiny, then how you react to life will reflect that story.

If the story you tell is a story that articulates your unique and vital role that you're here to play on the planet and fully expresses the preciousness of who you are; is unlimited and expansive, curious and wonder-filled, peaceful and sustainable, then what you create with your life will reflect that story.

Your story matters.

The prophecy of Ra Uru Hu and Human Design teaches us that we are on the cusp of a massive creative revolution. We are facing a series of global challenges that could threaten the well-being of all life on the planet. And yet, during this time when we need to tap into our innate creative power at our highest level, we are struggling with a massive crisis in creativity.

The metrics for creativity have been significantly declining over the last three decades. The Torrance Tests of Creative Thinking, used for decades by researchers to measure creativity and divergent thinking, are a better predictor of real-world success than traditional IQ tests. Researchers at William & Mary analyzed 300,000 Torrance scores since the 1950s and found that creativity scores began to nosedive in 1990.

People who know how to reactivate their innate creative power—people like you—will lead the world and build the future. They will know, through regaining control over the space between stimulus and response, how to harness life's intelligence and mine it for solutions.

But we can't see the solutions or occupy the information field that is the solution if we don't embody the story of the solution. You literally must *be* the change you want to see in the world.

To create abundantly, we must tell a story that is abundant. To be sustainable, we must first *be* sustainable, and so on.

If we look at the Human Design chart as a blueprint for the highest potential of the human story, we see that we are designed to be creative, sustainable, abundant, compassionate, empowered, loved, loving, and valued. Conditioning takes us away from our natural state.

Conditioning also causes us to use our vital life force to sustain the facade of a story that goes against our natural state. It actually takes energy to try to be someone you're not, to say yes when you want to say no, and to say no when you want to say yes to life.

The more control we assume over our own story, the more energy we liberate, making us more resilient and immune to burnout.

By taking back control of the story, you tell about who you are; you rewire your brain; you untangle yourself from stories that don't fit you anymore; and you start to create in a way that is truer to your nature. You become creative, sustainable, abundant, compassionate, empowered, loved, loving—and you heal your self-worth.

This is a lifelong journey of self-discovery. Take it slow. Make it a deeply personal process. Own it and shape it deliberately and with clear intention. It's a journey that starts first with your story.

Make it a good one.

ACKNOWLEDGMENTS

This book never would have happened without the prompting of my publisher, Randy Davila, who kept begging me to write a book about Human Design that was simple and easy to understand. His constant reassurance that it could be done kept me writing and from going down too many rabbit holes.

This book also never would have happened without the support, love, and ceaseless cheerleading from my team: Kristin, Jamie, Betsy, and Cindy helped me create countless images, double-checked my spelling, and endured my whining.

Aubri Parker helped me complete a large section of the book, including the chapter on Centers. Thank you for your steadfast and gentle brilliance.

Finally, thank you to all my students, my community, and my readers. It continues to be the most humbling honor to serve in the love army with you all.

APPENDIX

Life Purpose Statement Template

I, _____ (name), a _____
(your Human Design Type), am here to serve the world by _____
_____ (your Human Design Purpose).

I need, learn, share, and grow in my ability to give to the world through _____
_____ (conscious line of your Profile). I
need _____ (unconscious line of your
Profile) to be able to do so.

My affirmations for Defined and Open Centers:

Head: _____

Ajna: _____

Throat: _____

G-Center: _____

Will: _____

Emotional Solar Plexus: _____

Spleen: _____

Sacral: _____

Root: _____

I powerfully and passionately declare that my life purpose is to:
_____ (conscious Sun ☉ Gate theme)
and _____ (unconscious Sun ☉ Gate theme).

To do this, I allow, create, and receive _____ (conscious
Earth ⊕ theme) and _____ (unconscious
Earth ⊕ theme) as part of the foundation of the deep well of creativity that I am.

My early life experience brings me opportunities to learn and embrace
_____ (South Node ☋ —Personality Gate theme)
and _____ (South Node ☋ —Design Gate theme).

I look forward to keeping these lessons and experiences to help me fully lean into
_____ (North Node ☊ —Personality Gate theme) and
_____ (North Node ☊ —Design Gate theme), as I
mature in my essence and expression around age forty-four. I know the Universe
brings me opportunities so that I may learn to embrace and love all parts of me,
and I align with my essence as I grow, learn, and share with the world.

My heart and soul are driven by _____ (conscious
Moon ☽ Gate theme) and _____ (unconscious Moon
☽ Gate theme). I know that nurturing this drive gives me the energy and passion
to continue to align myself with my purpose. I embrace the challenge as part of
my learning and growth process. I know that when I encounter an inner conflict,
it is a symptom of my own expansion and indicates that I am learning and growing. I am always doing it right. I am always growing and changing.

My personal learning energy teaches me _____
(Saturn ♄ —Personality Gate theme) and _____
(Saturn ♄ —Design Gate theme).

When I master my inner lessons, I am blessed by _____
(Jupiter ♃ —Personality Gate theme) and _____
(Jupiter ♃ —Design Gate theme).

My spiritual purpose and path is _____
(Neptune ♆ —Personality Gate theme) and _____
(Neptune ♆ —Design Gate theme).

I call on these energies when I am in need of greater alignment with my Purpose.
I know that I need to master _____
(Chiron ⚷ —Personality Gate theme) and _____
(Chiron ⚷ —Design Gate theme) to deepen what I am here to share with the world.

I use this knowledge and wisdom to communicate through _____

_____ (Mercury ☿ —Personality Gate theme) and

_____ (Mercury ☿ --Design Gate theme).

I value _____ (conscious Venus ♀)

and _____ (unconscious Venus ♀).

My life lessons have taught me that I'm willing to fight for_____

_____(conscious Mars ♂) and _____

_____ (unconscious Mars ♂).

I was born into a generation that will awaken others to _____

_____ (conscious Uranus ♅) and _____

(unconscious Uranus ♅).

And will learn these lessons through cycles of _____
(conscious and unconscious Pluto ♇).

I share the full expression of who I am with the world through these energies. I play a unique role in the evolution of humanity, and I have a vital and irreplaceable place in the divine order. I honor all of who I am, and I deeply and completely love and accept myself.

ABOUT THE AUTHOR

Karen Curry Parker is the best-selling author of multiple books and the creator of the Human Design for Everyone Training System and the Quantum Alignment System. She has been speaking, coaching, training, and podcasting on these topics for more than thirty-five years, touching more than a million lives around the world. Her core mission is to help people live the life they were designed to live by discovering who they are, what they are here to do, and how to activate their potential and authentic life path.

With degrees in nursing and journalism, Karen began her work as a midwife while also launching her own publishing company. Upon the birth of her children, she focused on coaching and educating parents. She then studied advanced energy psychology techniques such as EFT and Belief Re-patterning, as well as Human Design.

She blended all her training to create a new leading-edge coach training program called the Quantum Alignment System™. She is currently pursuing her PhD in integrative health and working on multiple new books.

The mother of eight children, Karen is a Manifesting Generator whose Sacral has led her to living on an organic hobby farm in a small town in Wisconsin with her husband and her youngest daughter.

San Antonio, TX
www.hierophantpublishing.com